Women in Government

Remarkable Women: Past and Present

Women in Government

Politicians, Lawmakers, Law Enforcers

Lesley James

RAINTREE
STECK-VAUGHN
PUBLISHERS

A Harcourt Company

Austin · New York
www.steck-vaughn.com

Published by Raintree Steck-Vaughn Publishers, an imprint of
Steck-Vaughn Company

CREATED IN ASSOCIATION WITH MEDIA PROJECTS INCORPORATED
C. Carter Smith, *Executive Editor*
Carter Smith III, *Managing Editor*
Lesley James, *Principal Writer*
Ana Deboo, *Project Editor*
Bernard Schleifer, *Art Director*
John Kern, *Cover Design*
Karen Covington, *Production Editor*

RAINTREE STECK-VAUGHN PUBLISHERS STAFF
Walter Kossmann, *Publishing Director*
Kathy DeVico, *Editor*
Richard Dooley, *Design Project Manager*

Photos on front cover, clockwise from top left: Eva Perón,
Eleanor Roosevelt, Indira Gandhi, Empress Theodora

Photos on cover page, top to bottom: Frances Perkins, Crystal Bird Fauset,
Alva Myrdal, Queen Isabella I

Acknowledgments listed on page 80 constitute part of this copyright page.

Library of Congress Cataloging-in-Publication Data
James, Lesley.
    Women government: politicians, lawmakers, law enforcers / Lesley James.
        p.   cm. — (Remarkable women: past and present)
    Summary: Brief biographies of notable women who have contributed significantly
to the fields of government and law, from Bella Abzug to Khaleda Zia.
    ISBN 0-8172-5730-6
    1. Women in politics—Biography Dictionaries, Juvenile. 2. Women politicians—
Biography Dictionaries, Juvenile. 3. Women heads of state—Biography Dictionaries,
Juvenile. 4. Women legislators—Biography Dictionaries, Juvenile. 5. Women political
activists—Biography Dictionaries, Juvenile. [1. Women in politics. 2. Politicians.
3. Heads of state. 4. Legislators. 5. Political activists. 6. Women—Biography.]
I. Title. II. Series: Remarkable women.
HQ1236.J35   2000
920.72—dc21   99-20571
[B]   CIP
Printed and bound in the United States
1 2 3 4 5 6 7 8 9 0 LB 03 02 01 00 99

ADZ-3013

C O N T E N T S

INTRODUCTION

A S YOU READ THIS BOOK, IT IS QUITE LIKELY THAT YOU WILL NOTICE THE same thing that William Shakespeare observed four centuries ago in his play *King Henry IV*, part II: "Uneasy lies the head that wears the crown." This is true for an actual crown-wearing monarch struggling to hold out against rebellious subjects or powerful invaders. It's also true for a senator who was elected by a landslide but can't manage to muster up enough votes from the fickle public the next time around. The story of a notable political figure's career doesn't always have a happy ending. However, it takes a compelling personality to command, and you will meet plenty of such personalities in these pages.

Although history has obscured the accomplishments of women in other fields, we do have records of a number of impressive women rulers. This is partly because monarchy, the system by which the throne is inherited, was the custom for so long and in so many places. A princess might not have been first in line for the throne, but if she had no brothers, she would be crowned. Queen Elizabeth I, one of England's most respected monarchs, began her reign after her younger brother and then her older sister died while in power.

Another time-honored way for a woman to exercise control is through a husband or son who rightfully possesses the throne. In ancient Rome Agrippina kept a tight hold on her son Nero. In the 12th century, Eleanor of Aquitaine married first the king of France and then the king of England, strongly influencing both countries. In 20th-century America, First Lady Eleanor Roosevelt became one of the most beloved figures in history and established her own political presence while assisting her husband.

Often physical courage and ruthlessness go with the territory. The great warrior queens, like Boudicca and Raziyya rode with their troops into battle; their deeds became legendary. Wu Chao of China and Livia of Rome are believed to have plotted the deaths of even their own family members to fulfill their ambitions.

Over time many governments have followed the example of the United States and adopted some version of the democratic process for choosing leaders. Interestingly, though, constitutional democracies, by doing away with inherited power, at first actually allowed women *less* opportunity to participate in government than before. As a result aspiring female politicians joined the ranks of the reformers, fighting for universal suffrage and civil rights. In 1922 Rebecca Felton was symbolically placed in a senatorial seat during the off-season but finagled one full day of attendance once the government reconvened. In 1931 Hattie Caraway inherited a seat in the Senate and then won it for herself at the next election. And in 1978 Nancy Kassebaum became the first woman to win a seat in the Senate without following in a man's footsteps. Today, although men still outnumber them, women are increasingly involved in all areas of the government, and many people think a woman president is in our not-too-distant future.

Remember, many of the women you will read about here are still in mid-career. Their stories continue to unfold, and new women's stories begin every day. If you find that you are curious about what Justice Sandra Day O'Connor decided in the latest Supreme Court case, or what Mary Robinson is doing as the United Nations High Commissioner for Human Rights, or who is likely to be that first woman president, keep an eye on the newspapers.

Photos top left Jane Matilda Bolin, bottom left Liliuokalani,
top right Hillary Rodham Clinton, bottom right Barbara Charline Jordan.

Bella Savitsky Abzug (1920–1998)
United States congresswoman, lawyer

KNOWN FOR HER FEARLESS POLITICAL CRUSADES, her flamboyant personality, and her wide-brimmed hats, Bella Abzug was the first Jewish woman on Capitol Hill. Throughout her career as a lawyer, congresswoman, and activist, she inspired her supporters and aggravated her opponents.

After earning a law degree in 1947, she specialized in labor and civil rights. She defended underprivileged and oppressed clients, including those accused of "subversive activities" by Senator Joseph McCarthy during his anti-Communist campaign. She was one of the first lawyers to refer to the First Amendment, which guarantees the rights to free speech, press, and association. In addition, Abzug was a driving force in political movements, such as women's rights, nuclear disarmament, and affordable housing and day care. She was especially committed to ending the war in Vietnam.

In 1970 Abzug ran for Congress. Her loud, raspy voice, knuckle-cracking handshake, and no-nonsense attitude gained her attention from the national media. Although "Battling Bella" drove some voters away with her aggressive commitment to controversial issues, she won her seat in a landslide victory. Abzug brought the same enthusiasm that had characterized her campaign to the House of Representatives. Throughout her six-year term, she struggled to improve the system. On her very first day in Congress, she stood up to propose a resolution to bring American soldiers home from Indochina. She was not afraid to openly criticize presidents or organize demonstrations on the steps of the Capitol to make her points. After leaving Congress, she remained an active public figure. Her book, *Gender Gap: Abzug's Guide to Political Power for Women* was published in 1984.

Abigail Smith Adams (1744–1818)
First lady of the United States

WHEN HER HUSBAND, JOHN ADAMS, LEFT HIS family in Boston to attend the first Continental Congress in 1774, Abigail Adams's career as a letter-writer began. In addition to managing the family farm with great success, Abigail wrote letters that advised her husband on the constructing of a new nation. She took on "unladylike" issues, such as racial discrimination and the inequality of education for boys and girls (she had received no formal schooling herself, but had been an "eager gatherer" of learning). Her engaging letters described topics as diverse as a bloody battle, the meaning of "liberty," or how she was running low on pins.

Abigail joined John in Europe during his time as a foreign minister, but she continued to manage the

> "I cannot say, that I think you are very generous to the ladies; for, whilst you are proclaiming peace and good-will to men, emancipating all nations, you insist upon retaining an absolute power over wives. But you must remember, that arbitrary power is like most other things which are very hard, very liable to be broken; and, notwithstanding all your wise laws and maxims, we have it in our power, not only to free ourselves, but to subdue our masters, and, without violence, throw both your natural and legal authority at our feet."
>
> ABIGAIL ADAMS
> Letter to John Adams, May 7, 1776

farm by letter and passed on vivid pictures of life in the Old World to family and friends back home. When John became the first vice-president and then the second president of the United States, Abigail continued to offer him advice. It's debated just how much she helped to run the country, but there is no doubt she knew her mind and was not afraid to speak it.

After losing the election of 1800, the Adamses returned to Massachusetts, where Abigail devoted herself to running the farm, caring for her children and grandchildren, and guiding the career of her oldest son, John Quincy Adams, who would become the sixth president of the United States.

Mahnaz Afkhami (1941–)
Iranian stateswoman, women's rights activist

MAHNAZ AFKHAMI WAS BORN IN KERMAN, IRAN, and grew up during a time of modernization for the country's traditional Islamic inhabitants. In a strictly observant Muslim household, a woman wouldn't have been allowed to attend the University of Colorado for graduate work, but Afkhami did.

Back home by 1967, Afkhami taught English at the National University of Iran in Tehran. She also started a career in politics and activism. Leading the way in the fight for women's rights, she directed the Women's Organization of Iran. This led to her appointment to government positions. In 1974 she became a member of the government's High Council for Welfare and, two years later, was named minister of state for women's affairs. She served as a delegate to several United Nations conferences.

When the Islamic Revolution occurred in 1979, however, Afkhami's posts were eliminated. Religious fundamentalists seized control of the government. Many of the political rights and social freedoms Iranian women had won were taken away by decree. Once again, if a woman didn't cover her face with the traditional veil, she could be punished. Afkhami was forced to leave her homeland, but her voice continues to be heard. A noted author and editor, her publications include *Women in Exile* (1994). She is executive director of the Sisterhood Is Global Institute and the Foundation for Iranian Studies, and she is active with Human Rights Watch. She currently lives in Maryland.

Agrippina the Younger (15–59)
Roman empress

AGRIPPINA II CAME OF AGE IN THE DECIDEDLY dangerous environment of the Roman court, where she learned not only to survive political intrigue, but also to use her ambition and wit to create intrigue of her own. She was determined to become the ruler of the Roman Empire.

After her first husband, Domitius, died in the year 37, Agrippina was accused of treason and banished by her brother, the emperor Caligula. But his successor, Claudius, brought her back and fell so deeply under her influence that he married her. Agrippina's power is illustrated by the fact that Celtic captives brought to the Roman court ignored Claudius and bowed before the empress, assuming she was the one in charge.

Agrippina made sure that her son, Nero, would be heir to the throne, getting rid of all his rivals and possibly even murdering Claudius to speed the succession. Once he was on the throne, Nero was appalled at the way his mother steadily cultivated and increased her power. He finally put a stop to her ambition by having her killed.

Madeleine Korbel Albright (1937–)
Secretary of State of the United States

MADELEINE ALBRIGHT DESCRIBES HERSELF AS a woman first. She then adds that she's a Democrat, an international affairs specialist, a university professor, and the mother of three daughters.

She worked behind the scenes for years promoting Democratic causes and serving as the hostess of an informal salon for foreign policy experts. In 1993 she entered the limelight when President Bill Clinton made her American ambassador to the United Nations.

Albright was born in Prague, Czechoslovakia, and because her family was Jewish, lived in England during World War II. In 1948, when Communists took over the Czech government, her diplomat father asked the United States for political asylum. Albright spent her high school years in Colorado, went to Wellesley College, and then earned her Ph.D. at Columbia University in 1976. Because of her heritage, she chose to specialize in Eastern European and Russian affairs and became an advocate for democracy in those regions.

Albright was a well-liked professor at Georgetown University in Washington, D.C., during the 1980s and early 1990s. At the same time, she became steadily more involved in politics. She advised American presidential candidates, as well as Vaclav Havel, the first president of the newly liberated Czechoslovakia. During her years as an ambassador, her genuine warmth and humanitarianism won her consistent praise. In 1997 she became the country's first female secretary of state.

As the first woman on Ohio's Supreme Court and in a federal court of appeals, Allen proved that a woman was just as capable in the role of a judge as a man. She paved the way for women to serve on the United States Supreme Court, although she never attained that position herself.

Florence Ellinwood Allen (1884–1966)
Judge

FLORENCE ALLEN STARTED LAW SCHOOL AT THE University of Chicago but soon moved to New York City, where she lived at Maud Wood Park's Henry Street Settlement and campaigned for women's suffrage while attending New York University. Then, law degree in hand, she moved to Ohio, where she passed the state bar exam in 1914.

Allen continued her activism, providing free legal services to the Legal Aid Society and to Cleveland's suffragists. In 1920 she was elected judge of the Court of Common Pleas of Cuyahoga County. She did so well that she left the job two years into her six-year term, because she had been appointed to the Ohio Supreme Court. Then, in 1934, President Franklin Roosevelt made her a judge on the United States Court of Appeals for the Sixth Circuit. She served until her retirement in 1959.

Corazon Cojuangco Aquino (1933–)
President of the Philippines

CORAZON AQUINO LED A NONVIOLENT "PEOPLE power" movement, ending a 20-year dictatorship in the Philippines and becoming that country's first woman president. The original destiny of this shy, unassuming woman was to be a traditional wife and mother. In 1954 she married Benigno Aquino, a successful politician and a staunch opponent of the dictator Ferdinand Marcos. But Benigno was arrested for his defiance in 1972, and his years of imprisonment changed Corazon's life. She became his spokesperson and link to the world outside. After his release, the Aquinos went into exile in the United States. When Benigno decided to return home in 1983, he was gunned down at the Manila airport.

As a widow Corazon became a powerful symbol of resistance and was begged by the outraged Filipinos to run for president in 1985. Some thought she was too inexperienced to govern, but she won the hearts of the people by speaking to them as a fellow victim.

Aquino was elected despite the violence and

deceit Marcos used against her, and after thousands of loyalists carried out a peaceful demonstration of support. She was faced with the formidable task of restoring a nation ravaged by corruption, but through shrewd choices she brought about peace and economic revitalization. She decided not to run again in 1992, and the candidate she favored, Fidel Ramos, became the new president.

Dame Mary Arden (1947–)
Judge of the British High Court

MARY ARDEN BROKE NEW GROUND IN THE demanding field of company (corporate) law when she became the first woman to serve on Great Britain's High Court as a member of the Chancery Division, which deals with business. Arden, whose grandfather, father, and brother also went into law, grew up in Liverpool, England. She studied at Girton College, Cambridge, and spent a year in America on a fellowship at Harvard University in Massachusetts.

In 1971 Arden became a barrister, a lawyer who is authorized to bring cases before the British higher courts. There were few women barristers at the time, and none at all in the field of company law, but she achieved great success as a consultant in London's financial and legal world. In 1986 she received the title of "Queen's Counsel" in honor of her superior expertise. Upon her 1993 appointment as a High

Court judge, she was also made a Dame of the British Empire. Although the British judicial system is notoriously resistant to change, Justice Arden has introduced measures to reform and simplify many of the procedures used in the Chancery Division.

Artemisia I (5th century B.C.E.)
Queen of Halicarnassus

ARTEMISIA I IS THE FIRST WOMAN TO APPEAR IN historical records as a naval captain. She ruled the Anatolian coastal city of Halicarnassus, as well as Cos, a nearby island. The whole region was under control of the Persian king, Xerxes I, to whom she paid tribute money.

In 480 B.C.E. Xerxes invaded Greece, and Artemisia supported him with a five-ship fleet in what is now called the Battle of Salamis. She displayed exceptional courage and skill, but the battle was, nevertheless, a humiliating defeat for the Persian forces. The historian Herodotus, who was himself from Halicarnassus, reported that Xerxes eventually retreated to safety upon the advice of Artemisia. If he had not done so, his armies would have been completely destroyed. The Greeks offered a huge reward for Artemisia's capture, but she kept her life and her freedom.

Hanan Ashrawi (1946–)
Palestinian diplomat, political activist

PALESTINE IS A REGION OF SHIFTING BOUNDARIES with historical and religious significance to Arabs, Jews, and Christians. After the state of Israel was formed in 1948, the Arabs—now known as Palestinians—and the Jews clashed over ownership of lands, particularly in the West Bank, the birthplace and home of Hanan Ashrawi. By 1967 the West Bank was under Israeli control, and many Palestinians had lost their homes and rights.

Ashrawi is a powerful voice for those who wish to see Palestinian self-government restored by negotiation rather than military force. Beginning her career as a literature scholar, she was a professor at Bir Zeit University and became dean of the art school there. However, increasingly violent incidents in the West Bank during the 1980s drew her attention to politics. Sympathetic to the Palestine Liberation Organization (PLO), the main opposition to Israeli domination, Ashrawi appeared on American news shows and met with political figures such as Secretary of State James Baker. Her intelligence and gift for diplomacy attracted supporters from all over the world to her cause. In 1991 she represented Palestine as part of an advisory team at the Madrid conference, an attempt to negotiate peace. However, in spite of the positive results they achieved and the even more promising agreement made in Oslo, Norway, two years later, peace has still not been reached. Ashrawi continues her campaign, and she is currently a cabinet adviser to the Palestinian leader, Yasir Arafat.

Lady Nancy Astor (1879–1964)
Member of the British Parliament

VIRGINIA-BORN NANCY ASTOR STARTED LIFE AS A southern belle but ended up the first female member of the English Parliament. She was made of contradictions: quarrelsome but charming, wealthy but a defender of the poor, a political conservative but a champion of equal rights for women in work and marriage.

In 1906 Nancy married Waldorf Astor, a member of the House of Commons. He inherited his father's title in 1919, becoming a viscount, a level of nobility that is just above a baron and below an earl. It was then necessary for him to serve in the House of Lords, and Nancy was elected to fill his seat in the Commons. She

> "Women are young at politics, but they are old at suffering; soon they will learn that through politics they can prevent some kinds of suffering. They will face the political issue as they have faced all others when called upon; few men have tried their mothers and found them wanting, and nearly all men have tried their mothers at some time."
>
> LADY NANCY ASTOR
> *My Two Countries*, 1923

soon proved her commitment to the feminist cause, a loyalty based not on liberal politics but on the heartfelt desire to right wrongs. She believed the law did not sufficiently protect women and children and fought to change it, supporting widows' pensions, birth control, and stronger penalties for child abuse. A temperance advocate, she was a major force behind establishing 18 as the legal drinking age. Her dramatic ways sometimes angered other feminists, other members of the Conservative party, and certainly other members of Parliament, who resented this "invasion" by a female.

Katherine Stewart-Murray, Duchess of Atholl (1874–1960)
Member of British Parliament

KATHERINE, DUCHESS OF ATHOLL, WAS INVOLVED in public service long before she entered politics. In 1909 she was elected president of the local Red Cross Society in Perthshire, Scotland. During World War I, she turned her family castle into a hospital. So when she made her bid in 1923 to become the first Scottish woman in Parliament, she easily won the election. Honest and hardworking, she was sometimes disliked for her unwillingness to compromise on matters such as poor children's right to an education. Although not a supporter of women's suffrage, she consistently fought the exploitation of women, or of any group of people.

The duchess left Parliament after 1938, but she remained active. As World War II progressed, she sheltered European refugees and children evacuated from London. She also translated Hitler's *Mein Kampf* (My Struggle), hoping to warn the world of the danger the fascist German leader posed. Her own writings include *Women and Politics*, published in 1931.

Anita Augspurg (1857–1943)
Lawyer, political activist

ANITA AUGSPURG'S FAMILY BELIEVED THAT AN intelligent young woman should become a schoolteacher, not an actress or photographer, certainly not a lawyer or political activist. But as soon as she was able, Augspurg tried all of these careers—except schoolteacher—finding her true calling as a defender of women's legal rights. Since women could not attend university in Germany in 1893, Augspurg studied law at the university in Zurich, Switzerland. Returning to Germany as the country's first woman lawyer, she used her expertise and theater training to sway audiences, lobby the government, and found organizations to promote women's suffrage.

Although her style of feminism was termed "militant," Augspurg was opposed to military expansion and believed the women's and peace movements should work hand-in-hand. During World War I, she organized a Women's Peace Conference in the Dutch city of The Hague. The vote was granted to German women in 1919, and Augspurg continued to campaign for civil rights. When Hitler came into power in 1933, she fled to Zurich and remained there until the end of her life.

Aung San Suu Kyi (1945–)
Cofounder of Myanmar's National League for Democracy party

FOR HER COURAGEOUS EFFORTS ON BEHALF OF THE pro-democracy movement in Myanmar (formerly Burma), Aung San Suu Kyi has been awarded many prizes, including the Nobel Peace Prize for 1991. Her father, Aung San, led the movement that

gained Burma its freedom from British rule in 1948 and was assassinated when Suu Kyi was only two.

Although she lived abroad after 1960, Suu Kyi remained aware of the plight of her homeland, which was seized in 1962 by an oppressive military dictator, Ne Win. Inspired by the teachings of the Indian nationalist leader Mohandas Gandhi and influenced by her bond with the father she never knew, she prepared herself to return and serve her people someday. This return came in 1988, when she realized she could not remain a bystander while thousands of innocent protesters were brutally murdered or imprisoned. While her husband and two sons stayed at their home in England, Suu Kyi traveled to the land of her birth.

Suu Kyi gave focus to an otherwise disorganized movement in Myanmar. Her National League for Democracy demanded respect for human rights, condemning the military's abuse of power and advocating reconciliation. She traveled widely, rallying the people to nonviolent revolution. As unrest grew and political activity was banned, Suu Kyi and her followers were harassed and nearly killed. In July 1989, Suu Kyi was placed under house arrest, surrounded by guards and seldom able to see her family. She was offered permission to leave the country if she would refrain from political activities abroad, but she always refused. Although officially freed in 1995, she remains in Myanmar, certain that if she left she couldn't return. The military government has yet to relinquish control, even though the National League for Democracy won parliamentary elections in 1990 by a landslide.

Sirimavo Ratwatte Bandaranaike (1916–)
Prime minister of Ceylon

Chandrika Bandaranaike Kumaratunga (1945–)
President of Sri Lanka

Sirimavo Bandaranaike's husband, Solomon, the prime minister of Ceylon, was assassinated in 1959. After the tragedy Bandaranaike campaigned for her late husband's party, although she didn't seek office for herself. However, when the party won the election in 1960, she was appointed prime minister. Although her opponents labeled her a novice with no experience except as a homemaker, she had long been involved in women's welfare reforms and had received a political education from her husband.

Bandaranaike instituted nationalist programs, but her task was a very difficult one. The country had received partial independence from Great Britain in 1948, and it became a fully self-governing republic in 1972, when the name was changed to Sri Lanka. However, unemployment, hunger, and the ethnic and religious rivalry between the majority Sinhalese Buddhists and the minority Tamil Hindus kept the island in turmoil. Bandaranaike lost her popular support and, consequently, her office when the conservative United National party (UNP) came into power in 1977.

Meanwhile, Bandaranaike's daughter, Chandrika, had been raised in the political arena. She and her husband, Vijaya Kumaratunga, became leading figures in the opposition to the UNP. One of their main goals was a peaceful resolution to discrimination against the Tamils, who were conducting a guerrilla war against the government. Kumaratunga lost her husband the same way she lost her father: Vijaya was assassinated in 1988.

By 1994 disillusionment with the UNP had set in. Kumaratunga's new People's Alliance gained popularity, pledging to help the poor, seek negotiations with the Tamils, and encourage "capitalism with a human face." She was hailed as a catalyst for change, appointed prime minister, and then elected president. She then reappointed her mother prime minister, and the two continue to work together to satisfy both sides of the ethnic struggle in the midst of an ongoing civil war.

A Jewish Homeland

When Miriam Ben-Porat began her career, Israel was not yet an independent Jewish nation. Moving there, she joined a growing number of Zionists, Jews who wished to return to the land that had been theirs in biblical times. The area, which was better known as Palestine, had been under British rule since 1918, but the British were sympathetic to the Zionists' plans. In 1948, following World War II, the State of Israel was created, in spite of the opposition of the country's mostly Muslim neighbors. Over 50 years later, Israel is still working to achieve a lasting peace with them.

Mary Bartelme (1866–1954)
Juvenile court judge

One of the social reformers to come out of the Progressive Era was Mary Bartelme, who used her knowledge of law to change the way young girls accused of crimes were treated by the courts. Bartelme's interest in reforming the legal system was based on her belief that children were not inherently bad, but only neglected and in need of moral instruction and appropriate activities.

After years of private law practice in her native Chicago, Bartelme was appointed Cook County public guardian, in which role she helped establish a special court for juveniles and, in 1911, she was appointed assistant to the juvenile court judge. She heard delinquent girls' cases in private and attempted to help them, rather than just punish, although she did send many to reformatories. Journalists and lawyers alike praised her "court of another chance."

As assistant, Bartelme's recommendations were influential, but she had no judicial power of her own until she was elected judge of the Cook County Juvenile Court in 1923. She held the position until she retired ten years later. Bartelme was also known for the residential halfway houses she established for delinquent girls, the first such in her own home.

Miriam Ben-Porat (1918–)

Justice of the Supreme Court of Israel,
state comptroller

MIRIAM SHINEZON WAS RAISED IN A JEWISH community in Lithuania but chose to immigrate to Israel when she was 18, narrowly escaping the Holocaust. Once there, she took the surname Ben-Porat, and enrolled as a law student at Hebrew University in Jerusalem.

Ben-Porat began working in the state attorney's office in 1949. She soon established a reputation for being a relentless prosecutor and a stickler for proper procedure. This last quality antagonized her fellow lawyers, but her record was impressive. She went on to become deputy state attorney and district court judge. In 1977 she was the first woman appointed to Israel's Supreme Court.

After her mandatory retirement in 1988, Ben-Porat became the first woman state comptroller. Her job was to monitor the financial practices of government agencies and report to the public. She has had no problem accusing politicians and corporations of waste, corruption, and abuse of power. Along the way she has, naturally, displeased many influential people, but she retains her position because of the public's appreciation of her integrity in applying the law equally to all segments of society.

Benazir Bhutto (1953–)

Prime minister of Pakistan

THE MOST IMPORTANT PERSON in Benazir Bhutto's life was her father, Zulfikar Ali Bhutto, Pakistan's first democratically elected president. He was arrested following a military coup and executed in 1979. But he had taught his daughter to be a leader, as willing to make sacrifices for the country as he was. She would become Pakistan's first female prime minister, facing many of the same hardships that her father had.

After Zulfikar's death Benazir and her mother, Nusrat, led his outlawed Pakistan People's party in opposing the brutal regime of Mohammad Zia ul-Haq. Bhutto suffered in prison, went abroad to seek support, and returned to Pakistan in 1986, receiving a tremendous welcome from the people. In 1988 she decided to run for Parliament. Zia and his supporters tried to derail her campaign. Among the obstacles they contrived was scheduling the election for the day she was due to give birth. But the baby was born early, and Bhutto was elected to the National Assembly, then appointed prime minister.

The people looked to Bhutto to fulfill her promises and replace authoritarian rule with a socialist program. She faced many challenges: civil war, the resentment of Islamic fundamentalists for the leadership of a progressive woman, and charges of favoritism toward family members. Bhutto was prime minister until 1990 and served again from 1993 to 1996. She did much to restore civil liberties and champion the poor, but hers was an uphill battle that was never won.

Shirley Temple Black (1928–)

Diplomat, child star

SHIRLEY TEMPLE, THE ADORABLY DIMPLED CHILD star of 1930s Hollywood, is famous around the world, but the adult she grew into—Shirley Temple Black, political activist and diplomat—is less well known. Not the first former movie actor to go into politics, she used her talents well in both professions.

Black first came into contact with politics during the Korean War while her husband, Charles, served at the Pentagon. Returning home to California, she ran for Congress in a special election in 1967. She lost the race, probably due to her pro-Vietnam War stance, but continued to work for the Republican party, promoting other candidates. In addition, she sat on the committees of many community service organizations and lobbied for a reduction of the voting age from 21 to 18, believing that young people must get involved as soon as possible, to prepare for their future roles as leaders.

In 1969 President Richard Nixon included Black in a five-member delegation to the United Nations General Assembly, and in 1974 she served as the American ambassador to Ghana. She became chief of protocol in the State Department under Gerald Ford two years later, a position ideally suited to her extraordinary charm and poise.

Blanche of Castile (1188–1252)
Queen of France

THE DAUGHTER, WIFE, AND MOTHER OF KINGS, Blanche of Castile proved to be an able ruler in her own right. Her father was Alfonso VIII of Castile, and her mother, Eleanor, was the daughter of Henry II of England. Blanche was 11 when her powerful grandmother, Eleanor of Aquitaine, arranged for her to marry the heir to the French throne.

Louis VIII was crowned in 1233 but died only three years later. Blanche then ruled on behalf of their 12-year-old son, Louis IX. When troublesome nobles contested his claim to the throne, she led troops into battle, dressed in white and riding a white horse. Among her greatest achievements was concluding the Treaty of Paris in 1229, which calmed civil unrest and led to an extended and prosperous peace in France.

After Louis turned 21, Blanche no longer ruled officially, but her influence on him kept her very much involved. In 1248 she once again became regent so that Louis could go on a crusade to the Holy Land. When Louis was captured by the Turks, Blanche negotiated his release, but she died before he returned home.

Jane Matilda Bolin (1908–)
Judge

JANE BOLIN BECAME THE FIRST AFRICAN AMERICAN woman judge when Mayor Fiorello LaGuardia appointed her to the Domestic Relations Court of New York City in 1939. It was a fitting achievement for the first black woman graduate of Yale Law School. After passing the state bar in 1932, she had practiced with her husband, Ralph Mizelle, and served as assistant corporate counsel in the city's law department, where she focused on racial discrimination in employment.

When Bolin joined the Domestic Relations Court, she made a point of drawing attention to discrimination in the schools. She used her authority to fight for racial justice and earned respect and praise for her compassion, common sense, and—incidentally—her beauty. After a long career with few decisions reversed by higher courts, Bolin retired in 1978. She continued to be active in urban and African American organizations, volunteering with children and seeking to improve race relations.

Boudicca (1st century, died 62)
Celtic queen

BOUDICCA, WARRIOR QUEEN OF THE ICENI, A CELTIC tribe of eastern Britain, led her people in a revolt against the colonizing Romans in the year 61. Contemporary reports say she was very tall, with a long mane of bright red hair. Her passion inspired her people and terrified her enemies.

After her husband, Prasutagus, died, Roman overlords attacked Boudicca, raped her daughters, and stole her land. Smoldering resentment burst into flame and drove Boudicca to seek revenge. She had no trouble rallying the people to follow her into battle. It was not uncommon for a Celtic woman to rule or fight.

Boudicca waited until the Roman governor was at battle far away. Then she struck with ferocity,

destroying Roman settlements and killing 70,000 people. The Roman troops couldn't believe an army that included so many women had thoroughly defeated them. The result of the devastation was a temporary liberation for the Celts, but the governor soon returned. Boudicca and her army were defeated the next year.

There are differing reports of her death. Some traditions hold that she died in combat; others, that she swallowed poison rather than be taken prisoner; still others say she survived the battle but died of disease soon after. Despite the final defeat, Roman rule in Britain was less severe following the rebellion.

Barbara Levy Boxer (1940–)
United States congresswoman

THE 1992 ELECTIONS RESULTED IN A DRAMATIC increase in the number of women elected to serve in the Senate. Barbara Boxer, a Democrat from California, was one of them. She attributed her victory to her ability to work cooperatively without compromising her beliefs and to growing awareness among voters that women's lack of power is linked to their absence from high political offices.

Boxer has overcome many obstacles based on her sex. At high school in Brooklyn, New York, she wasn't allowed to play on the baseball team, so she coached it instead. She began her career as a stockbroker, even though she had to struggle to find a firm willing to hire a woman for that job. By the mid-1960s, Boxer was married and living in California. Sharing the activist mood of the country, she became involved in local politics in spite of being criticized for working outside the home.

Her efforts were rewarded when she was elected to the House of Representatives in 1983. Ten years later, she defeated more prominent opponents to win a seat in the Senate. Throughout her career, Boxer has fought for environmental protection, education, health care, and child welfare. She has opposed wasteful military spending and taken a tough stand on crime.

Gro Harlem Brundtland (1939–)
Prime minister of Norway, physician

GRO HARLEM BRUNDTLAND REALIZED EARLY ON that, as a doctor, she could only help a few patients at a time, but as a politician she could help an entire country, even the world. She believes that political decisions must incorporate scientific knowledge and that promoting good health is the key to economic development.

After obtaining degrees from the Oslo University Medical School and Harvard University, Brundtland began a career in public health. In 1974 she was appointed minister of the environment. Her power increased rapidly: Six years after entering the cabinet, she was elected Norway's first woman prime minister. Her term lasted only eight months, but she was reelected in 1986 and in 1990, finally resigning in 1996. While in office, she assembled the world's first gender-balanced government, appointing seven women to high positions in her 18-member cabinet.

As a Labor party leader, her fortunes depended on her party's popularity. Her husband belonged to the opposing Conservative party, but he always supported her personally. Her work on behalf of world health and environmental issues won her praise abroad, but Norway's persistent economic problems often earned her criticism at home. She has served on many global committees. Most recently, she was named the first woman leader of the World Health Organization.

Brunhilde (550?–613)
Frankish queen

DURING THE SIXTH CENTURY, THE KINGDOM OF THE Franks, which roughly corresponds to modern France, was divided into smaller territories that were ruled by the sons of whichever king managed to eliminate his brothers and seize command. The sons, in turn, tried to eliminate one another. For nearly 40 years, Queen Brunhilde played a role in this brutal struggle. Some historians consider her a power-hungry tyrant. Others describe a skillful and devoted queen, a patron of the arts and of the new Catholic church.

In 567 Brunhilde married one Frankish king, Sigebert I of Austrasia, and her sister married his brother, King Chilperic I of Neustria. Soon after, Brunhilde's sister was murdered at the instigation of a rival, Fredegund, who then married Chilperic.

A bitter hatred arose between Brunhilde and Fredegund. It would lead to conspiracies, murders, even all-out war. Husbands and sons perished in course of the feud, but Brunhilde and Fredegund endured, each leading her army into battle and acting as regent for her sons or grandsons. Fredegund died in 598, and Brunhilde was not able to maintain her influence. In 613 rebellious Frankish nobles handed her over to Fredegund's son, Chlotar II, who ordered her tortured and then dragged to death behind a wild horse.

Jane Burke Byrne (1934–)
Mayor of Chicago

JANE BYRNE JOINED THE NOTORIOUS "CHICAGO Democratic machine" as a protégée and loyal supporter of Mayor Richard Daley, whom she met after working on John F. Kennedy's presidential campaign. He appointed her to positions in the Democratic party and in city government, where she

made an impression—and enemies—by aggressively rooting out corruption and criticizing other officials for disloyalty to Daley. When Daley died in 1976, Byrne's enemies took away much of her power. Within a few months, Daley's successor, Michael Bilandic, removed her altogether.

Accusing Bilandic of dishonesty and inefficiency, Byrne challenged him in the mayoral race of 1979. The odds were against her: she had never held elected office. But then the "Blizzard of '79" paralyzed the city under nearly two feet of snow, and Bilandic was blamed for the city services' failure to deal effectively with the disaster. Byrne used the situation to her advantage and won the election with more votes than Daley had ever received. Byrne spent two terms in office. Among her focuses were working to improve housing and schools and getting rid of "dead weight" employees by not playing favorites.

Kim Campbell (1947–)
Prime minister of Canada

KIM CAMPBELL'S AMBITION AND PASSION FOR politics reached a peak when she became the first woman prime minister of Canada. A graduate of the University of British Columbia law school, she was relatively new to the national political scene. She spent most of the 1980s working in local Vancouver politics. Then, in 1988, she joined the Progressive Conservative (Tory) party and was elected to the House of Commons.

Campbell dealt successfully with controversial issues. She was responsible for the passage of a strong gun control law in 1991, and her unpretentious and often irreverent manner made her popular. Even though she was a conservative, she did not hesitate to stand up for women's and minority's rights. Most importantly, she became the protégée of Prime Minister Brian Mulroney.

In 1993 Mulroney, whose popularity had plummeted in the wake of economic decline, stepped down, and Campbell was chosen to replace him until the next election. With her fresh ideas and energy, she rallied some support in her campaign to win the seat for herself, but not enough. Along with most other Tory candidates, Campbell lost the parliamentary race just four months later.

Hattie Wyatt Caraway (1878–1950)
United States congresswoman

Hattie Caraway was the first woman elected to the United States Senate. As a ceremonial gesture, the Arkansas governor appointed Caraway to take her husband Thaddeus's place as senator after he died in 1931. She was only supposed to occupy the seat until a special election could be held, but she surprised everyone by winning the special election, winning a full term in 1932, and another in 1938.

Although her experience in politics had been limited to supporting her husband's career, Caraway took her new duties seriously and performed them well. She served in several important posts, and in 1932 became the first woman to sit in for the president of the Senate. A supporter of President Franklin D. Roosevelt, she was in favor of his New Deal. She also took a strong interest in agricultural issues and voted for Prohibition. She was a sponsor of the Equal Rights Amendment when it was brought before the Senate in 1943. Caraway was a comfortable, "motherly" figure, as thoroughly capable of serving her country as she had been of running a cotton plantation and taking care of her family.

Cartimandua (1st century)
Celtic queen

Cartimandua, queen of the Celtic tribe the Brigantes, presided over the largest realm in first-century Britain. She tried unsuccessfully to maintain her kingdom by making allies of the increasingly powerful Romans. When they invaded in the year 43, she signed a treaty with them. But this decision was so unpopular that she had to call on the Romans to defend her from revolts by her own people. To show her loyalty to the Romans, she betrayed her fellow Celtic ruler, Caratacus.

Cartimandua's marriage was also a source of political trouble to her. Venutius acted alternately like a beloved husband and an adversary for the throne. He tried to incite the people to overthrow Cartimandua and make him king in 57. Afterward the two ruled together peacefully, but only for a short while.

Finally Cartimandua eloped with her husband's armor-bearer, Vellocatus, thereby losing the support of everyone. Following a bloody battle in 71, the Brigantes's land became a part of the Roman Empire.

Catherine de Médicis (1519–1589)
Queen of France

Catherine de Médicis wielded great power as regent of France. She built a centralized government securely controlled by the monarchy and instituted some reforms. But her determined pursuit of these goals—and her desire to ensure that her sons inherited the throne—led her to use not only underhanded methods, but to initiate outright civil war.

Catherine belonged to the great Médici family of Florence, Italy. In 1533 she was married to France's

The Médicis of Florence

From the 15th to the 18th centuries, the Médicis were among the most powerful families in Italy. They controlled Florence and, later, Tuscany. Four became popes, and several besides Catherine married royalty. With roots in the peasant class, they gained influence through the family businesses: cloth manufacturing and banking. Often they were despotic rulers, but they were extraordinarily enlightened about cultural matters. Florence became a center for art, architecture, and learning. Anna Maria Luisa, the last of the line, died in 1743 and bequeathed the family art collection, housed in a spectacular building, to the city. It is called the Uffizi Gallery.

future King Henry II, who ascended the throne in 1547. She tried to be a good wife, but Henry ignored her. He was in love with Diane de Poitiers and took her counsel in all things. Wisely, Catherine made a friend of Diane. When Henry died in 1559, Catherine came to power as regent for her first and second sons, Francis II and Charles IX, both of whom died young. Henry III, her third son, ruled on his own, although still with her assistance.

As regent Catherine faced many serious challenges: an empty treasury, threat of war, noble families attempting to seize power, and a bitter feud between the Catholics and the Protestant Huguenots. Whether she acted out of ignorance, self-interest, or a true attempt to bring about peace, Catherine was responsible for the tragic St. Bartholomew's Day Massacre on August 23, 1572, during which 70,000 Huguenots were killed.

Catherine II (1729–1796)
Empress of Russia

BRILLIANT AND RUTHLESS, CATHERINE THE GREAT transformed Russia from a barely civilized country into a powerful empire with lasting influence on European politics. In 1744 she was chosen by the formidable Empress Elizabeth I of Russia to be the future bride of her son, Peter. Leaving her home in Prussia, Catherine traveled to St. Petersburg. The 15-year-old princess pleased Elizabeth by embracing all things Russian, learning the language, and converting to the Orthodox faith. She overlooked the many deficiencies of the Russian courtiers, who were not only rude but often unclean—even lice-ridden. She also tried to like her fiancé, whose only passion was for toy soldiers.

Despite Catherine's efforts, the marriage wasn't a success. Peter neglected her, and she read French philosophers. When Peter became czar, he managed to offend everyone with his eccentric behavior. Catherine, on the other hand, had many supporters. In 1762 she dressed in a soldier's uniform and rallied the army to her side. Before he knew what was happening, Peter was a prisoner in his own home, and within a week, he was dead. Catherine would rule Russia as an "enlightened despot" for the next 32 years.

Catherine thought of herself as a progressive ruler: she made many reforms, was a patron of the arts, and greatly expanded Russia's frontiers through diplomacy and military victories. Yet, for all her ambitions, her accomplishments were not always practical. Many were killed in her wars, and the lowest classes—the serfs—lost even more power and freedom. On her death, Catherine left her son, Paul I, a vast empire but one sown with the seeds of revolution.

Violeta Barrios de Chamorro (1929–)
President of Nicaragua

FROM 1933 TO 1979, NICARAGUA WAS RULED BY the Somoza family, whose corrupt military regime aroused fierce opposition among the people. Violeta Chamorro's husband, Pedro, was one such rebel. As the publisher of a newspaper called *La Prensa* (The Press), he printed articles criticizing the dictators and calling for a democracy. He was arrested, banished, and, in the end, assassinated. Then Chamorro, whose role had been to care for the family and bring her husband food in prison, stepped into the political spotlight.

Chamorro supported the Marxist Sandinistas, who sought to bring down the Somozas. They succeeded in 1979, and Daniel Ortega Saavedra came to power. However, their repressive measures strongly

The Iran-Contra Affair

The United States' involvement in the conflict between the Sandinistas and the Contras led to a serious political scandal. At the time, Muslim terrorists were holding several Americans hostage in Iran. Hoping to free them, Robert McFarlane of the National Security Council (NSC) sold weapons to the Muslims, even though U.S. policy forbade negotiation with terrorists. Another NSC staff member, Oliver North, sent the Contras some of the money from the arms sales, also a violation of policy. Both situations came to light in 1986, and the public was outraged. In the ensuing trials, it became apparent that President Ronald Reagan's administration was aware of the transfers.

resembled those of the administration they had replaced. Chamorro soon broke her ties to the government. Civil war erupted between the Sandinistas and the United States–backed rebels, the Contras. Again, this time under Violeta's management, *La Prensa* ran articles that opposed the military rule, despite censorship and harassment.

In 1990 Chamorro ran for president. She was certainly not a slick, practiced politician, but her actions had made her positions clear. She had plenty of ardent supporters. As one newspaper remarked, "She doesn't have to talk; she can just lead the procession." Once elected, the country's first female president showed impressive independence of mind, negotiating a truce and restoring civil rights. She remained in office until 1996 and, in spite of continuing opposition by the Sandinistas, did much to bring peace and democracy to her country.

Mary Eugenia Charles (1919–)
Prime minister of Dominica

THE CARIBBEAN ISLAND NATION OF DOMINICA HAS endured political scandal, corruption, and hurricanes, but with Eugenia Charles as its first woman prime minister, it moved toward stability. The granddaughter of a former slave, she earned her law degree at the University of Toronto and practiced for a time in England.

When Charles returned home to Dominica in 1949, she was the first woman lawyer in her country. Concerned by the abuses and mismanagement that plagued the Labor party, she joined the rival Freedom party and eventually became its leader. As a member of the House of Assembly, she helped defeat the Labor government. Her party, which received support from both rich and poor because of its integrity and unity, won the elections of 1980 by a large margin, making Charles the new prime minister.

Charles led Dominica toward democracy, instituted reforms and social welfare programs, and helped revive agriculture and industry. She dealt with several conspiracies against her administration. In 1983, when militant leftists overthrew the government in neighboring Grenada, Charles's request for intervention from the United States received criticism, but she stood by her decision. She was reelected two years later and served for another decade, retiring in 1995.

Chiang Ch'ing (1913?–1991)
Communist leader, Madame Mao Tse-tung

CHIANG CH'ING BECAME ONE OF THE MOST powerful women in Communist China through her fiery support of her husband, Mao Tse-tung. Chiang met Mao in 1936. He was already a powerful leader of the Chinese Communist party, and she was an actress with an undistinguished career. They married despite the party's disapproval.

In 1949 the Communists triumphed over the Nationalists, and the People's Republic of China was born. For years Chiang obeyed party orders and supported Mao from behind the scenes. In 1963 she began to play a more prominent role when Mao assigned her the task of reforming the arts in preparation for the Cultural Revolution. This "revolution within a revolution" replaced established power structures despite violent resistance. Chiang rose steadily in the party ranks. She became a cultural dictator whose speeches could inspire crowds of Red Guards, topple public officials from power, and eliminate any art that wasn't true to Mao's principles.

The Cultural Revolution slowed in 1969, and Chiang became less influential, although she retained power by acting on behalf of her aging husband. Ten days after Mao's death in 1976, Chiang's political enemies arrested her, along with three other officials who implemented Mao's Cultural Revolution—they are now known as the infamous "Gang of Four."

Charged with undermining the government and torturing innocent citizens, Chiang was sentenced to death in 1980, then given life imprisonment. Her death was reportedly a suicide.

Shirley St. Hill Chisholm (1924–)
United States congresswoman

SHIRLEY CHISHOLM, THE FIRST AFRICAN AMERICAN woman ever elected to Congress, felt that a woman in politics meant a woman in office, not helping out at campaigns by stuffing envelopes. Born in Brooklyn, New York, she spent her early childhood with her beloved grandmother on a farm in Barbados. After returning to New York, she became an authority on early education and child welfare. She became increasingly involved in politics and reform groups, including the NAACP and the League of Women Voters. In 1964 she ran for a seat in the New York State Assembly and won.

Although she designated herself a Democrat, Chisholm emphasized that she ran by public demand, not with the backing of a political party. She knew the people of her Brooklyn district personally and understood their problems. She was able to address her Puerto Rican audiences in Spanish. In the assembly her direct, honest style won even more support and, in 1968, using the campaign slogan "Unbought and Unbossed," she was elected to Congress. During her 14 years on Capitol Hill, she devoted herself to promoting equal rights for women, people of color, the young, the poor, the unemployed, and the handicapped. She criticized the Vietnam War and supported the Equal Rights Amendment. Her bid for the presidency in 1972 was unsuccessful, but just by entering the race, she proved that finally the system was changing for the better.

Christina (1626–1689)
Queen of Sweden

MORE A PHILOSOPHER THAN A POLITICIAN, Queen Christina of Sweden was a disciple of the great French thinker René Descartes. In search of an answer regarding the nature of love, she wrote to Descartes, and they struck up a lively correspondence. Eventually, she invited him to be her personal tutor. He agreed to come to Stockholm, and also to the queen's insistence that their lessons be held at five in the morning, when her mind was free and clear. To Christina's sorrow, Descartes died in 1650, only five months after he arrived.

During her reign, which began in 1644, Christina brought about positive changes in education and industry, as well as ending the Thirty Years' War. However, she began to concentrate on other matters than those of state. In 1654 Christina secretly

Three Decades of Strife

The Thirty Years' War began in 1618 as a struggle between Roman Catholics and Protestants in Bohemia and Austria. It sparked related fights for religious and territorial reasons and drew in many European countries. Among other events, Denmark attempted to seize land from Germany; Poland attacked Russia and Sweden; Spain lost control of the Netherlands; and France annexed parts of Alsace and Lorraine. The 1648 Peace of Westphalia brought the conflict to an end, although an uneasy one. Queen Christina is considered one of the strongest forces behind the agreement.

converted to Roman Catholicism, which was forbidden in Sweden, then abdicated the throne.

She moved to Rome, devoting herself to the world of ideas and art. She enjoyed the company of brilliant friends and wrote literary works of her own. Somewhat late in the day, she once again became interested in politics and attempted to take control of Naples and of Poland. Subsequent attempts to reclaim the Swedish crown were thwarted by the state ministers who disliked her religion and her way of life. Without bitterness, though, she returned to Rome and there spent her final days.

Tansu Çiller (1946–)
Prime minister of Turkey

TANSU ÇILLER WAS NOT ONLY TURKEY'S FIRST female prime minister, but the first woman to lead a predominantly Muslim country who hadn't followed in her father's footsteps. Instead, she was seen as a symbol of change from the old system of government, with which many Turks were dissatisfied.

Çiller was born in Istanbul to a family who made a point of giving her a western education. She went to America for college and eventually earned a Ph.D. in economics from Yale University. Returning to Turkey in 1974, Çiller taught until she joined the conservative True Path party, which came to power in 1991.

Prime minister Süleyman Demirel made Çiller minister of the economy. Two years later, when he became president, she was elected prime minister. Her economic plans were controversial, and she found it difficult to keep her campaign promises, such as instituting constitutional reforms to make the country more liberal and democratic. Çiller's time in office was plagued by the collapse of the Turkish currency and stock market, opposition from religious fundamentalists, and ethnic conflict within Turkey and in neighboring countries. In 1997 she stepped down.

Cleopatra VII (69–30 B.C.E.)
Queen of Egypt

DESPITE HER REPUTATION FOR RUTHLESS AMBITION, murder, and seduction, Cleopatra VII was a good queen, devoted to her country. She is known

more for her beauty and cruelty, less for her brilliance and interest in learning and the arts.

Cleopatra was a descendant of the Macedonian Greek general, Ptolemy, who had helped Alexander the Great to conquer Egypt. Her family had ruled for centuries. She ascended the throne when she was 17, while the country was in the middle of a civil war. Winning the support of the Roman emperor, Julius Caesar, she secured the throne. In the process, though, she fell in love and left Egypt, living with Caesar in Rome until his assassination in 44 B.C.E.

Back in Egypt, Cleopatra dreamed of ruling an empire. She sought another Roman ally and romantic partner in Mark Antony, her equal in passion and ambition. However, their military campaigns were unsuccessful, and their loss of the sea battle at Actium in 31 B.C.E. meant the end of their dreams. Cleopatra was captured by the Roman general Octavian. Antony, mistakenly believing that she was dead, killed himself. Cleopatra attempted to win over Octavian, but without her usual success. To avoid public humiliation, she also committed suicide, supposedly by allowing herself to be bitten by an asp.

Cleopatra and Antony were buried together. Had their schemes succeeded, they might indeed have ruled the world. Instead Rome annexed Egypt, and Cleopatra entered the halls of legend and romance.

Genevieve Rose Cline (1879–1959)
Judge

GENEVIEVE ROSE CLINE GAINED MUCH OF THE practical experience she needed to be a judge outside of school. After attending high school in her hometown, Warren, Ohio, and spending a year at Oberlin College, she began working as a clerk for her brother, John, a lawyer in Cleveland. She also participated energetically in city and state women's political organizations. Increasing her speaking skills through lobbying sessions in Congress, Cline addressed issues such as child labor and health care. In 1917 she enrolled as a law student at Baldwin-Wallace College in Cleveland. Afterward she continued to broaden her political experience, eventually becoming vice-president of the Ohio branch of the Women's National Republican Association.

In 1922 Cline was made appraiser of foreign merchandise in Cleveland. Six years later President Calvin Coolidge appointed her to the United States Customs Court in New York City, where she presided over cases involving imported merchandise. Other women had been judges on the state level, but Cline was the first federal judge. Hardworking and thorough, she remained in the post for 25 years.

Hillary Rodham Clinton (1947–)
First lady of the United States

SINCE HER HUSBAND BECAME PRESIDENT OF THE United States, Hillary Rodham Clinton has been an object of both admiration and criticism. Her opponents claim that she has been given too much political power, that the first lady shouldn't be a policy-maker. But her supporters point out that she is a talented, well-established lawyer in her own right, fully qualified to serve in a presidential administration.

After graduating from Yale Law School, Hillary worked with the Children's Defense Fund. Then she surprised her friends by turning down a prestigious job at a Washington law firm and following Bill Clinton to Arkansas, where they married in 1975. Their career as a political team began a year later, when Bill was elected attorney general. He became governor of Arkansas in 1978, but lost a reelection bid in 1980. This defeat made Hillary aware of the importance of public appearance. Fearing that her label as a radical feminist might have cost her husband the victory, she began transforming herself to project a more conventional, feminine image. In the very next gubernatorial election, Bill Clinton was returned to the office, and he remained there for five terms, until he was elected president in 1992.

During Bill Clinton's presidency, Hillary's public image has been a constant factor. She faced considerable opposition when her husband appointed her head of a committee to reform national health care. Like other working mothers of her generation, she continues to face the challenge of maintaining her career without appearing "anti-family."

Edith Campion Cresson (1934–)
Prime minister of France

EDITH CRESSON JOINED THE FRENCH SOCIALIST party in the early 1960s after meeting François Mitterand, the party leader. She would follow Mitterand as he climbed the political ladder, becoming one of his most trusted lieutenants.

In 1981, when Mitterand was elected president, he appointed Cresson minister of agriculture. She was the first woman in this position, and she immediately came into conflict with the French farmers, who nicknamed her "the perfumed one." To make matters more difficult, Cresson was outspoken, stubborn, and welcomed a good fight, qualities not considered feminine. Despite her unpopularity—more than once she was pelted with rotten fruit and mud—she managed to raise France's agricultural income. In 1983 she became trade minister and turned to promoting French industry. She commuted to work on French motor scooters to show that they were as well made as the Japanese competitors'. Unfortunately, she believed so strongly that Japan was France's enemy in an "economic war," that her criticisms of the Japanese bordered on racism.

Mitterand appointed Cresson prime minister in 1991. After ten months of battling France's economic problems and other politicians, she resigned under pressure. French feminists blamed sexist attacks by politicians and the media for her downfall. She has remained in the public eye, though. In 1995 she became a member of the European Commission, a committee that establishes legislative policy for the new European Union.

Bernadette Devlin (1947–)
Member of British Parliament, activist

BERNADETTE DEVLIN, A LEADER IN NORTHERN Ireland's civil rights movement, grew up in a poor Catholic family. As a scholarship student at Queen's University in Belfast, she began to question the militant ideas she had absorbed as a child. Traditional Republicans desired above all a united Catholic Ireland. Devlin became a socialist, promoting civil rights for all Irish people, Catholic and Protestant. She organized peaceful, non-religion-based demonstrations, which were often the target of police brutality.

Devlin had not planned to enter politics, but in 1969 she reluctantly agreed to stand for Parliament against pro-British Unionist party candidates. After a whirlwind campaign, the 21-year-old won the election. In a powerful first speech to the House of Commons, she condemned the British policy in Northern Ireland, calling for equal treatment for Catholics and an end to oppression.

That same year Devlin was accused of inciting riots and imprisoned for four months, although she insisted she had tried to prevent the violence. She lost her seat in Parliament in 1974. Eight years later a terrorist group, the Ulster Defense Association, attempted to assassinate her. Both Devlin and her husband, John McAliskey, survived serious wounds. She continues to speak out, but more quietly.

Doi Takako (1928–)
Member of the Japanese Parliament

DOI TAKAKO IS DIFFERENT FROM THE TRADITIONAL Japanese woman: Tall, outspoken, unmarried, and childless, she was the first woman to be elected chairperson of a Japanese political party. Because of the example she has set and her cultivation of the women's movement, many other Japanese women have run for office and won.

Doi was a law professor in 1969 when she decided to enter politics—after someone told her it would be stupid to run in parliamentary elections, since a woman couldn't win. She not only won that year, she kept on winning. Doi's eloquence impressed the people, even though she spoke in a husky voice instead of the high-pitched tone Japanese women are expected to use. The Socialist party elected her chairperson in 1986.

During the 1989 campaign, Doi voiced the people's dissatisfaction with the corrupt government led by the opposition party. A baseball fan who enjoyed singing karaoke and playing a pinball-style game called pachinko, she was known for her "common touch." Ironically, her outgoing "male" behavior attracted people to her party, which won the election, but even ardent supporters thought she was too unconventional to be prime minister. Doi stepped down as leader of the Socialist party in 1991, but returned to the post in 1997, at the request of her fellow party members.

Elizabeth Hanford Dole (1936–)
Politician, president of the American Red Cross

ELIZABETH DOLE IS KNOWN FOR HER OWN CAREER in public service and for her marriage to an equally prominent American politician, Senator Robert Dole of Kansas. After practicing law, Dole began her political career in 1967 as part of President Lyndon Johnson's "Great Society" program. Under Richard Nixon, she served in the Office of Consumer Affairs and on the Federal Trade Commission. Ronald Reagan appointed her secretary of transportation, making her the first woman to lead an armed service—she was in charge of the Coast Guard. She then headed the Labor Department under George Bush, but resigned after two years to become president of the American Red Cross.

Dole, a native of North Carolina, who trained at Harvard Law School, presents a genteel exterior but is known for her dedication to her work. She has been criticized for changing her views to please new administrations and for turning against the Equal Rights Amendment. But there are many people who believe that, rather than support her husband's presidential aspirations, Dole should seek that office for herself.

Elizabeth Domitien (1920?–)
Prime minister of the Central African Republic

ELIZABETH DOMITIEN LIVED IN THE SHADOW OF the unstable, power-mad Jean-Bedel Bokassa, dictator of the Central African Republic. A successful businesswoman, she was an influential spokesperson for Mouvement d'Évolution Sociale d'Afrique Noire (Social Evolution Movement of Black Africa), an equal rights organization that helped the Central African Republic achieve independence from France in 1958. Seven years later Bokassa ousted the president of the new republic in a military coup.

As a childhood friend of Bokassa's, Domitien benefited from the new regime, which was something of a roller-coaster ride. In return for supporting him, Bokassa advanced her business enterprises. In 1975 he appointed her prime minister, making her Africa's first woman to attain that post. But she was a "puppet" without real power and lost the position a year later. Chilling reports began to circulate that Bokassa enjoyed vast wealth while the people starved and that he executed anyone who spoke out against him, even children. In 1979 France helped to remove him. As a member of his cabinet, Domitien was arrested and imprisoned for two years. Little is known of her current activities.

Eleanor of Aquitaine (1122–1204)
Queen of France and England

ELEANOR OF AQUITAINE WAS ONE OF THE MOST powerful women of her day. At the age of 15, she inherited her father's vast domain of Aquitaine and married King Louis VII of France. She was much more intelligent than Louis, as well as charming, passionate, and strong-willed. While they were married, she influenced state decisions and went with him on a crusade, bringing along a company of women in specially made armor. During the crusade, her closeness to her uncle aroused Louis's jealousy, which led to an annulment of their marriage in 1152.

Eleanor got her lands back and chose Henry of Normandy, who soon became king of England, from her many eager suitors. Her 50-year reign was filled with intrigue. She supported her sons, Richard and John, in an attempt to overthrow their father. As punishment, she was imprisoned until Henry's death 15 years later. Immediately upon her release, she made a grand tour through England, winning the country's loyalty for her favorite son, Richard the Lionhearted. She ruled the country while Richard went on crusade, though she would have preferred to go with him. After Richard's death, she made sure her son John succeeded, then returned to Aquitaine.

Eleanor had great influence over the cultural life of her times. Musicians, poets, and scholars gathered at her court in Poitiers. She continued to protect her family and her lands until the age of 80. Then, understandably exhausted, she spent her last years in quiet retirement at the convent in Fontevrault.

Elizabeth I (1533–1603)
Queen of England

ELIZABETH I RULED ENGLAND FOR 45 YEARS. SHE protected the country without initiating war, maintained authority without losing the affection of her people, and kept the country from going

bankrupt in a time of turmoil. Her devoted subjects called her "Good Queen Bess."

Born in 1533, Elizabeth disappointed her parents by being a girl. This provided one of the excuses her father, King Henry VIII, needed to get rid of her mother, Anne Boleyn, whom he eventually had beheaded. With considerable intelligence as her protection, Elizabeth outlived her father, her frail younger brother, Edward VI, and her tyrannical older sister, Mary I. In 1558 the people rejoiced as she ascended the throne.

Everyone expected Elizabeth to marry and produce an heir. However, although she used the possibility of marriage as a lure to keep her many royal suitors in line, she remained single. The union Elizabeth cherished was that between queen and country. To marry would have meant sharing that power.

Elizabeth oversaw an era of commercial and artistic flowering, but it was also filled with tension. She tried to find a solution to the fierce hatred between Catholics and Protestants, but she was also a Protestant defending herself from Catholic plots. Her greatest moment was in 1588, when she led England to a naval victory over the Spanish Armada. After that bad harvests caused economic depression in the country, and she lost some popular support. Her favorite courtier, the earl of Essex, tried to lead a rebellion against her in 1601. Two years later she died, bringing the Elizabethan Age to an end.

the same rationing rules as their subjects, and, in Elizabeth's case, drove an army vehicle.

Elizabeth inherited the crown from her father in 1952. Despite her great wealth and status as the nation's figurehead, she prefers ordinary country life and is happiest wearing a tweed skirt and walking her dogs. She has done much to adapt her role to suit modern times. She is the first English monarch to pay income taxes. The failed marriage of her heir, Prince Charles, to the late Lady Diana also inspired criticism of the royal family, but Elizabeth's dignified and sincere personal image continues to inspire many.

Elizabeth II (1926–)
Queen of England

To BE QUEEN OF ENGLAND IN THE 20TH CENTURY is very different from being queen in the era of the first Elizabeth. Elizabeth II is a symbol, not a policy-maker, although she has stayed informed of what the policy-makers are up to. During her reign she has weathered violent conflicts abroad, domestic discontent, and family scandals.

Unlike Elizabeth I, the modern Elizabeth had a quiet childhood with lots of pets and loving parents. She didn't start life as a direct heir to the throne, but when her uncle, King Edward VIII, abdicated (renounced the throne) to marry the American divorcée Wallace Simpson, Elizabeth's father became George VI. During World War II, the royal family, already popular, became even more so because they remained in England despite the dangers, followed

Eugénie (1826–1920)
Empress of France

Eugénia María de Montijo de Guzmán, the daughter of the Spanish Count of Teba, was born in Granada during an earthquake. In 1853 she married the former Louis Napoléon, who was president of the Republic of France after 1848 and became Emperor Napoléon III when the monarchy was restored. Known for her beauty, Eugénie (as she was called in France) was skilled in the arts of society, not politics. She backed conservative causes, while Napoléon tried to lead France toward liberal democracy.

Nevertheless she was politically influential, because she ruled while Napoléon was away fighting the wars, which broke out frequently. She helped protect the pope's control of Rome after the rest of Italy was unified and was involved in the creation of the Mexican Empire. One progressive act was helping women gain entrance to medical schools.

Napoléon abdicated in 1870, after his defeat in the Franco-Prussian War, and moved with Eugénie to England, where he died. Eugénie hoped her son would claim his father's crown and encouraged him to gain experience by fighting in Africa, but he was killed in the process. She ended her days in exile but not isolation, continuing to exercise her famous charm to stay in the public eye.

Crystal Bird Fauset (1893–1965)
Pennsylvania state legislator, activist

CRYSTAL FAUSET WAS A CIVIL RIGHTS ACTIVIST, race relations expert, and the first black woman to be elected to a state legislature. As a member of many organizations, beginning with the YWCA in 1918, she developed her gift for public speaking by expressing the needs and achievements of blacks, and the need for people of all races to work together. She created an institute for race relations at Swarthmore College, became involved in Franklin Roosevelt's Works Progress Administration, and founded the Philadelphia Democratic Women's League. Because of her experience and talent, the Democratic party urged her to run for the Pennsylvania legislature in 1938.

After a tough battle, Fauset won a seat in a district that was two-thirds white. Her campaign issues were universal, not limited to race, a stance that gained her national recognition, especially among women voters. Fauset became a member of the influential "Black Cabinet," which advised Roosevelt on race relations, and she was also a close friend of Eleanor Roosevelt. Despite this connection, she switched her political affiliation to the Republican party in 1944, because she felt that the Democratic party's leaders discouraged

African American women from participating. After 1945 she focused on world affairs, traveling in India, the Middle East, and Africa as part of an intercultural race relations council.

Dianne Goldman Feinstein (1933–)
Mayor of San Francisco, United States congresswoman

DIANNE FEINSTEIN CAME TO PUBLIC ATTENTION in 1978, when, as president of the San Francisco Board of Supervisors, she told the press that Mayor George Moscone had been assassinated, along with her fellow supervisor, Harvey Milk. Feinstein had recently announced her retirement, but she changed her mind as she held the dying Milk in her arms.

Feinstein, a Stanford University graduate, began her career in various government agencies, with a focus on criminal justice. In 1969 she was the first woman elected to the Board of Supervisors. While there, she worked hard to understand the problems of other classes and cultures. After the assassinations, she served out the remainder of Moscone's term, then was elected mayor in her own right, a position she held for ten years. It was a time of emotional crisis, but she helped the city to work through it. She also took on the difficult job of encouraging the diverse communities of San Francisco to cooperate with one another, although her center-of-the-road approach often pleased neither conservatives nor liberals.

In 1990 Feinstein ran for governor of California, but her failure to support women's issues while mayor cost her the votes needed for victory. During her 1992 campaign for the United States Senate, however, she focused on the need for more women in Congress. She won that race and was reelected in 1994.

Rebecca Latimer Felton (1835–1930)
Political figure, social reformer

THE PEOPLE OF GEORGIA LISTENED WHEN REBECCA Felton spoke her mind. Through newspaper columns and speeches, she spoke out on many issues: prohibition of alcohol, education, prison reform, farmers' concerns, and women's rights. Unfortunately, she

wasn't so progressive in all areas and shared the bigotry of many of her contemporaries against people of different racial, ethnic, and religious backgrounds.

Rebecca Latimer married Dr. William Felton, a man with liberal political aspirations, in 1853. During the Civil War she supported the Confederates, cared for wounded soldiers, and endured many hardships. Her hatred of war and the "stupid, cruel men" who governed fueled her own political fires. In 1874 she served unofficially as her husband's campaign manager when he ran for Congress. During his second campaign, however, she was recognized openly as an accomplished public speaker and partner in her husband's political affairs.

At age 87, Felton became the first woman to sit in the United States Senate. She was asked to fill the seat of Thomas Watson, who had died during the Congressional recess. This was a symbolic appointment—by the time Congress met again, there would be an elected successor. But Felton persuaded the successor to delay his arrival for one day and used that time to make a speech about women's future in politics.

Miriam Ferguson (1875–1971)
Governor of Texas

MIRIAM "MA" FERGUSON MADE NO SECRET OF the fact that she was running for governor of Texas only because her husband couldn't. In 1917 James Ferguson had been impeached from the office for improper use of finances. Although previously opposed to women's suffrage, James actively campaigned for his wife in 1924, promising "Two Governors for the Price of One." The Fergusons' folksy appeal attracted support from poor farmers, despite his tarnished record.

Ma Ferguson shares the distinction of being America's first female governor with Nellie Tayloe Ross, who was elected in Wyoming the same day. Ferguson courted controversy by pardoning many convicts, including her husband. However, by drastically reducing spending, she brought Texas's budget from deficit to surplus, a remarkable feat considering that she did this during the Depression. She was an ardent opponent of the racist organization the Ku Klux Klan. A believer in the New Deal, Ferguson supported raising taxes to fund education and always tried to identify the needs of common citizens. She served a second term as mayor from 1932 to 1934.

Geraldine Ferraro (1935–)
United States congresswoman, vice-presidential candidate

GERALDINE FERRARO BEGAN WORKING AS AN assistant district attorney in the New York borough of Queens in 1974. Increasingly she became aware that the domestic violence cases she handled had their roots in deep, complex social issues, such as poverty and discrimination. Feeling that she couldn't do enough to solve these problems as a prosecutor, she ran for the House of Representatives in 1978 and won.

In Congress Ferraro worked hard for her district of working-class people and retirees. She also cosponsored the Economic Equity Act in 1981, designed to achieve equal pay for women—an injustice she had experienced herself in a previous job. She managed to take a strong stand on women's issues without alienating male colleagues.

In 1984 the Democratic candidate for president, Walter Mondale, named Ferraro as his running mate. She was chosen for her talent and hard work, her devotion to the Democratic party, and her popularity with voters. For the first time ever, a woman was on a major political party's ticket as a vice-presidential candidate. During the elections, Ferraro weathered accusations of mishandling family finances and of being a party favorite without enough experience. Although she and Mondale lost the election, Ferraro showed how far women politicians have come—and how far they still have to go. She remains in the public eye. In 1992 and 1998 she ran unsuccessfully for a seat in the United States Senate. Between those elections she served as a member of the United Nations Human Rights Commission, then cohosted *Crossfire*, a political talk show on the Cable News Network.

Vigdis Finnbogadóttir (1930–)
President of Iceland

A S A WELL-KNOWN TELEVISION PERSONALITY AND expert on Icelandic culture, Vigdis Finnbogadóttir was well suited to be president, a position that, in Iceland, calls for a cultural ambassador rather than a policy-maker. After she was elected in 1980, "President Vigdis" impressed many other world leaders with her intelligence, charm, Nordic beauty, and fierce pride in her country.

Before entering politics, Vigdis acted as a guide for foreign journalists, directed the Reykjavik Theater Company, and lectured about Icelandic culture and literature. She ran for president to prove that a woman could win and hold the post. She certainly made her point, remaining in office until 1997. She is considered one of the best representatives that Iceland has ever had.

As president Vigdis spoke out about environmental issues and women's rights. In 1985 women all over the country staged a strike to protest discrimination and demand equal pay. It was feared that the absence of the striking flight attendants would disrupt air traffic, one of Iceland's most important sources of income. Vigdis was forced to sign a bill forbidding them to strike. But the flight attendants walked out anyway—and she followed them.

Elizabeth ("Betty") Bloomer Ford (1918–)
First lady of the United States

A S A YOUNG WOMAN, BETTY BLOOMER ASPIRED TO be a dancer and spent several years away from her home in Grand Rapids, Michigan, performing with Martha Graham's company in New York City. She married Gerald Ford in 1948, expecting to settle into the calm, orderly life of a lawyer's wife. Instead Gerald, an active Republican, immediately ran for the United States House of Representatives and was elected. In 1973 the developing Watergate scandal propelled him into the vice presidency and—upon Richard Nixon's resignation—the presidency.

Betty made the best of the situation, speaking out in support of the Equal Rights Amendment and other controversial issues, as well as championing the arts and child welfare organizations. Gradually, though, she was overwhelmed by the strain of constantly being on public view, nurturing her four children, suffering from crippling back pain, and, worst of all, recovering from breast cancer.

The Fords left the White House in 1977, when Gerald lost the presidential election to Democrat Jimmy Carter. Betty checked into a substance abuse clinic the next year. She was as frank about her battle to overcome alcohol and drug addiction as she had been about her breast cancer operation. As a result she inspired many people to take action for their own problems. In 1982 she founded the alcohol and drug rehabilitation center that bears her name.

Indira Nehru Gandhi (1917–1984)
Prime minister of India

INDIRA GANDHI, INDIA'S FIRST WOMAN PRIME minister, was respected for her determination to bring democracy and peace to a country torn apart by intense fighting between religious and political groups. Unfortunately, her reputation was marred by the questionable methods she used to stay in power.

Her father was Jawaharlal Nehru, an important figure, with Mohandas Gandhi (no relation to Indira), in the struggle to free India from British rule. She was inspired by her parents' commitment to their cause, even though she was frequently separated from them when they were imprisoned. By the age of 12, she had established the Monkey Brigade, an organization of 1,000 children who spied on the unsuspecting British.

In 1947 India became an independent nation, with Nehru as its first prime minister. Gandhi served as her father's adviser and assistant. By the time of his death in 1964, she was already president of the Indian National Congress, the country's most important political party. Two years later, she became prime minister. Through her leadership, she improved international relations and instituted reforms intended to wipe out poverty. However, during riots, Gandhi declared states of emergency that limited personal freedom, imprisoned political opponents, and censored the press. During a state of emergency in 1984, Gandhi forcefully suppressed a

revolt by extremist members of a religious sect called the Sikhs. Later that year, she was assassinated by two of her bodyguards, Sikhs who resented the way she had handled the uprising.

Ruth Bader Ginsburg (1933–)
Justice of the United States Supreme Court

RUTH BADER GINSBURG OVERCAME QUITE A FEW obstacles to become a lawyer, but she only realized later that she had experienced sexual discrimination. At Harvard Law School, the dean asked the new women students why they were taking spots that could have been given to men. After transferring to Columbia University, she graduated at the top of her class but still had trouble finding work. It was during the 1960s, when the American Civil Liberties Union referred sex discrimination cases to her, that she considered her experiences in feminist terms. From then on, she focused on bringing about social change and became increasingly influential in her field.

In 1972 Ginsburg became the first tenured woman professor at Columbia Law School and cofounded the ACLU's Women's Rights Project. President Jimmy Carter appointed her to the United States Court of Appeals for the District of Columbia in 1980. In 1993 President Bill Clinton nominated her for the Supreme Court. Her appointment was overwhelmingly approved by the Senate, a tribute to her impressive career and fair decisions. Only the second woman to serve as a Supreme Court justice—Sandra Day O'Connor was first—she has taken a moderate approach, believing that sweeping changes are less effective than gradual but convincing ones.

Pamela Harriman (1920–1997)
Political hostess, ambassador to France

PAMELA HARRIMAN BROUGHT IMPORTANT PEOPLE together, raised funds, and chaired campaigns. She drew her political power from the men she loved, married, or supported until quite late in her colorful, adventurous life, when she finally came into her own.

The daughter of an English baron, Pamela Digby married Winston Churchill's son Randolph at the start

of World War II. Their marriage soon failed, but Pamela got along fine with her father-in-law, who became prime minister in 1940. As his companion, she survived the trials of the war and met world leaders. During this time, she began a notorious series of romances with powerful men, such as journalist Edward R. Murrow, rich French vintner (wine-maker) Baron Elie de Rothschild, and singer Frank Sinatra.

During the 1950s Pamela worked as a journalist in Paris and played hostess to artists, intellectuals, and celebrities. On a visit to New York City, she met Leland Hayward, a Broadway producer, whom she married in 1960. After he died, she encountered an old wartime flame, W. Averell Harriman, former governor of New York, presidential adviser, and millionaire. They married, and Pamela threw all her energy into supporting his party, the Democrats. So successful were her "issues dinners" and "political action committees" that some credit her for helping to bring the party back into power with the election of Bill Clinton. As a reward, Clinton named her ambassador to France in 1993. She was at her post in Paris when she died at age 76.

Penny Harrington (1943–)
Chief of police

P ENNY HARRINGTON DECIDED TO BE A POLICE officer when she visited a police station for a high school field trip in her hometown of Lansing, Michigan. In 1966 she got her first job, working in the juvenile division of the Portland, Oregon, police force. She advanced steadily, but along the way she had to file 42 civil suits against the department for discriminatory practices. Finally, in January 1985, she became the first woman police chief of a major American city.

Harrington worked to improve relations with the Portland community, initiating cultural awareness

training for officers. She also encountered budget cutbacks, full jails, and resistance to change. The crisis came when a black man died while being subdued by white officers. Harrington fired two other white officers for reacting insensitively to the event, which brought praise from community leaders but caused an uproar within the force. After a police union hearing obligated her to rehire the men, increasing criticism of her policies caused her to resign in 1986. She is now the director of the National Center for Women and Policing, based in Los Angeles, California.

Marcelite Jordan Harris (1943–)
Air Force general

I N HER DISTINGUISHED MILITARY CAREER, MARCELITE Harris has achieved numerous firsts and won many awards, all of which led to her becoming the first black woman in the Air Force to achieve the rank of general. Born in Houston, Texas, Harris studied speech and drama at Spelman College in Georgia. In 1965, the year after she graduated, she enrolled in the officer training school at Lackland Air Force Base, Texas.

In the years that followed, Harris performed impressively at posts in California, Germany, Illinois, Colorado, Kansas, Japan, and Mississippi. She was stationed in Thailand during the Vietnam War and served as a White House social aide to President Jimmy Carter in 1975. In 1990 she was made a brigadier general and the vice-commander of the Oklahoma City Air Logistics Center at Tinker Air Force Base. She was promoted to major general in 1995 and, until her retirement two years later, served as director of maintenance at the Air Force Headquarters in Washington, D.C.

Mary Belle Harris (1874–1957)
Prison superintendent

M ARY BELLE HARRIS DISCOVERED HER CALLING as a prison administrator somewhat late in life. Originally a classics scholar, she studied at several universities and spent time working abroad. Then, when she was 40 years old, she accepted a job in New York City at the Blackwell Island Workhouse

> "We must remember always that the 'doors of prisons swing both ways'; that most of their tenants are coming back to the community to sit beside us in the street-cars, and beside the children of our families at the movies, with no bars between and no wall around them. Unless we have built within them a wall of self-respect, moral integrity, and a desire to be an asset to the community instead of a menace, we have not protected society—which is ourselves—from the criminal."
>
> MARY BELLE HARRIS
> *I Knew Them in Prison*, 1936

for women. Her success in transforming dangerous and depressing institutions would earn her a reputation as a miracle worker.

Harris encouraged a system of self-government that conferred responsibility on the inmates, who learned to be productive citizens. They were taught job skills to increase their self-respect and free them from dependence on men—and crime—for financial support. Harris's system, geared to the individual woman's needs, provided education, exercise, and leisure activities, such as reading and knitting. She insisted that a mostly female staff should guard her women prisoners.

Harris participated in the administration of various prisons and detention homes. Then, in 1925, she was hired to help plan and lead the Federal Industrial Institution for Women in Alderson, West Virginia. She served as superintendent there until she reached the mandatory retirement age of 65.

Patricia Roberts Harris (1924–1985)
Public official, lawyer

A NATIVE OF ILLINOIS, PATRICIA HARRIS STARTED life poor and ended up working to solve the problems of poor across the nation. Her varied and distinguished career reached its height when President Jimmy Carter appointed her Secretary of Housing and Urban Development in 1977, then Secretary of Health, Education, and Welfare two years later. A woman who—because of her race—

could not have bought a house when she first moved to Washington, D.C., became the first black woman to hold a Cabinet post.

From her days as a college student at Howard University, Harris was involved in the civil rights movement. After a career in human resources, she studied law at George Washington University. She joined the criminal division of the Justice Department and then the law faculty of Howard University. By 1969 she was a full professor.

In the meantime Harris had entered politics. President Lyndon Johnson appointed her the ambassador to Luxembourg in 1965. She was the first African American woman in that role. She also served on numerous human rights organizations, and sat on the board of directors of several corporations, believing corporate responsibility could speed social change. In 1982 she ran unsuccessfully against Marion Barry in the Washington, D.C., mayoral elections. Her death three years later was caused by cancer.

Beverly Harvard (1950–)
Chief of police

B EVERLY HARVARD WAS ALWAYS INTERESTED IN helping people. In 1972 she graduated with a degree in sociology from Morris Brown College in Atlanta, Georgia. She never considered joining the police force, though, until one day her husband, Jimmy, bet her that she couldn't pass the rigorous entrance tests. As she went through the tough physical and mental training, she found her calling—and won $100 from the bet.

Many other challenges followed. Harvard spent two years on street patrol, during which time she had to convince her husband that she didn't need a bodyguard in tough neighborhoods. She earned a reputation among her superiors for having good ideas for improving the department. Steadily, she moved up to become an affirmative-action specialist, the director of public affairs, and then deputy police chief. In 1994 the mayor of Atlanta, Bill Campbell, promoted her to the top, making her the first African American woman police chief of a major city. Harvard has used her talent for calming controversy and her gift for administration to reach out to officers and the community they serve, significantly improving relations between the two.

Hatshepsut
(late 16th–early 15th century B.C.E.)
Queen of Egypt

HATSHEPSUT TOOK CONTROL OF EGYPT AFTER THE deaths of her father and husband, when she became regent to her nephew, Pharaoh Thutmose III. The boy came of age, but Hatshepsut refused to relinquish her power. She announced that they would share the throne, claiming that Amon-Re—Egypt's most powerful god—had appeared to her in a dream to reveal that he was her true father. To reinforce her position, she often appeared in public wearing male clothing, including the false beard that was, by tradition, worn only by pharaohs.

During her successful 20-year reign, Hatshepsut brought prosperity to Egypt through trade and agriculture. Working with her architect, Senmut, she built impressive monuments and imported treasures from distant lands to adorn them. Thutmose grew increasingly impatient with her refusal to let him take command. After her death, which is believed to have occurred between 1484 and 1458 B.C.E., he took out his frustration on her memorials, ordering the destruction of many of them in an attempt to erase her name from history.

Hino Tomiko (1440–1496)
Ruled as a Japanese shogun

BORN IN KYOTO INTO THE HIGHEST SOCIAL RANK in Japan, the noble class, Hino Tomiko traded her social status for power. She became a member of the warrior class by marrying a shogun (a military governor), Ashikaga Yoshimasa, in 1455. She went on to give birth to two daughters. The Shogun, fearing that his family would sacrifice its power without a male heir, adopted his brother, Yoshimi, to succeed him. But then Hino did, after all, have a son, Yoshihisa. She worked busily at securing his right to rule as shogun, which led to the bitter 11-year-long Onin War against the supporters of the rejected Yoshimi.

Fortunately for Hino's purposes, her husband was weak and gradually withdrew from political and social life. Hino soon took over for good, ruling in her son's name. Using cleverness and ingenuity, she collected a fortune through heavy taxes and financial speculation. When her son died in 1489, she established Yoshimi as the shogun and continued to rule through him.

Oveta Culp Hobby (1905–1995)
Army colonel, public official, newspaper publisher

OVETA CULP BEGAN WORKING IN GOVERNMENT at an early age. She was 20 when she became parliamentarian of the Texas House of Representatives. In 1931 she married the publisher of the *Houston Post* and former Texas governor, William Hobby. She took over many managerial roles at the *Post*. In time she would also become active in radio and television broadcasting, serve on many boards and commissions, and participate in politics and civic welfare groups.

During World War II, Hobby was appointed chief of the women's division of the Bureau of Public

> "Lo, the god knows me well,
> Amun, Lord of Thrones-of-the-Two-Lands;
> He made me rule Black Land and
> Red Land as reward,
> No one rebels against me in all lands.
> All foreign lands are my subjects,
> He placed my border at the limits of heaven,
> What Aten encircles labors for me."
>
> From an inscription on a monumental
> obelisk erected by HATSHEPSUT

Relations in the War Department. She developed plans for a women's auxiliary branch of the army, which later achieved full military status. She was given the relative rank of major, and later promoted to colonel. As director of the WAC, her responsibilities included enlisting and overseeing women volunteers in noncombat military posts.

After the war ended, Hobby continued her work in publishing and politics until President Dwight Eisenhower appointed her director of the Federal Security Administration. The FSA was soon redesignated the Department of Health, Education, and Welfare, and as its secretary, Hobby was the second female Cabinet member after Frances Perkins. While she occupied the post, Hobby investigated ways to alleviate the high costs of health care, but she opposed the institution of a nationalized system.

Isabella I (1451–1504)
Queen of Spain

IN 1469 THE AMBITIOUS PRINCESS ISABELLA, HEIR to the throne of Castile, secretly married Ferdinand, the heir to the throne of Aragon. It would prove to be a powerful union. By 1479 they ruled both lands, and their first task was to bring to heel the rebellious lords who had been allowed to run wild there. Isabella put codified laws to work in the previously lawless kingdom.

Isabella, a fervent Catholic, supported the Spanish Inquisition, created in 1478 by the pope to investigate and punish religious "crimes." The Jews and Islamic Moors who lived in Spain were deemed heretics. They were forced to convert to Catholicism or flee the land. The Inquisition achieved its goal of ensuring religious purity, and a strong Spanish cultural identity was established. The price, however, was high. Thousands were killed, and Spain isolated herself from many of the new ideas flourishing in the rest of Europe.

The year 1492 was a momentous one in Spanish history. After an 11-year campaign, Isabella and Ferdinand managed to drive the Moors from their stronghold of Granada, uniting all three Spanish kingdoms—Castile, Aragon, and Granada—for the first time in 800 years. They sent Christopher Columbus on the first of his voyages that led to the establishment of Spanish colonies in the New World. And the Jews were decisively expelled from Spain by the Inquisition.

The legacy of Isabella's far-reaching vision—which included conquering and converting as much of the world as her Spanish ships could reach—can be felt to this day around the globe.

Annie Baeta Jiagge (1918–1996)
Justice in Ghana's Court of Appeals

ANNIE JIAGGE BECAME GHANA'S FIRST WOMAN lawyer, judge, and then Supreme Court justice at a time when few Africans, much less African women, aspired to a law career. Jiagge was a schoolteacher in the 1940s when Ghana began to edge toward independence from England. Inspired, she decided to become a lawyer, and traveled to England to attend the best schools available. She earned her degree from the London School of Economics and qualified as a barrister. In 1950 she returned home to Accra to practice.

In 1957 Ghana achieved independence, and by 1961 Jiagge was a judge on the High Court. Eight years later, she was appointed to the Court of Appeals. As Ghana adjusted to its new status as a republic, Jiagge led the way toward reform and free elections, rooting out government corruption. Her efforts were felt abroad as well. She served as a representative on the World Council of Churches, the United Nations' Commission on the Status of Women, and many other organizations. Dignified and capable yet approachable, she was considered a remarkable judge and humanitarian.

Jito (645–703)
Empress of Japan

BORN IN 645, JITO WAS THE DAUGHTER OF THE Japanese emperor Tenji. When her father retired, her brother Kobun succeeded him in 671. However, Tenji's brother Oama had long planned to rule. He seized the throne within a year, declared himself Emperor Temmu, and sealed his claim by marrying Jito. After Temmu's death in 686, Jito assumed control and was formally proclaimed empress four years later. Stepping down in 697, she crowned her grandson Mommu emperor.

Jito was a skillful administrator. She completed and instituted Japan's first legal code, promoted agricultural interests, and issued the first silver coin. She strove to ensure harmony between Japan's two religions, Buddhism and Shintoism, contributing funds to both. In addition, she is remembered as a gifted poet.

Barbara Charline Jordan (1936–1996)
United States congresswoman, lawyer, educator

GROWING UP IN A POOR BUT SUPPORTIVE FAMILY, Barbara Jordan knew she wanted to do something meaningful and challenging with her life. She became a lawyer in her hometown of Houston, Texas, deciding that the best way to make the country a more just and equal place was to change legal and governmental systems from within. In order to help as many underprivileged people as possible, she ran for public office. In 1965 she became the first African American member of the Texas Senate since 1883—and Texas's first-ever black woman senator.

Jordan achieved the respect of her fellow senators while she fought for employment and anti-discrimination issues. In 1972 she was elected to Congress, where she continued to work on behalf of consumers, women, poor people, and students. Four years later she was the first woman to deliver the keynote speech at a Democratic National Convention. Jordan retired in 1978 and taught at the University of Texas at Austin until her death. She was the recipient of many awards and honors, including the 1994 Presidential Medal of Freedom.

Nancy Landon Kassebaum (1932–)
United States congresswoman

THERE WERE WOMEN IN THE SENATE BEFORE Nancy Kassebaum, but she was the first woman to be elected in her own right, instead of taking the place of a senator husband who had died in office. Kassebaum's father, Alf Landon, had challenged Franklin D. Roosevelt's bid for the presidency in 1936. Following his example, she entered the national political scene.

A divorced mother of four, Kassebaum had

helped to run her family's two radio stations, worked in Kansas politics, and served on the staff of Republican Senator James B. Pearson. After Pearson chose not to run again in 1978, she decided to try for his seat—and won by a substantial margin. Her views reflected the political attitude of her home state, but it was still unusual for conservative, rural voters to back a woman.

During her three terms in Congress, Kassebaum disappointed many feminists who felt her support of the Equal Rights Amendment and abortion rights was lukewarm. She was active on the Commerce and Foreign Relations Committees and was rumored to be a vice-presidential candidate in 1988. She did not seek reelection in 1996.

Jeane Jordan Kirkpatrick (1926–)
United Nations delegate, political scientist

JEANE KIRKPATRICK'S INFLUENTIAL CAREER HAS included teaching political science and serving as a consultant to the Departments of Defense; State; and Health, Education, and Welfare. She is a much-published writer and a respected scholar, although critics often disagree with her pro-American, pro-military stance and her fervent anti-communism.

The Oklahoma-born Kirkpatrick received much of her higher education in New York City, earning her B.A. from Barnard College and her Ph.D. from Columbia University. She went on to teach, and by 1968 had begun her long association with Georgetown University. Throughout the 1970s, Kirkpatrick was active in the Democratic party. She considered herself liberal on domestic issues such as welfare and organized labor. However, her stance on foreign policy was conservative. She viewed the anti-war, anti-establishment movement of the 1960s as idealistic and counterproductive. Increasingly, she saw President Jimmy Carter's foreign policy as expressive of that outlook, and she began to rethink her support of him.

In 1980 Kirkpatrick joined the campaign for the Republican presidential candidate, Ronald Reagan. After Reagan's election, she advised him on foreign policy, and he appointed her a permanent delegate to the United Nations. Although she defended many of Reagan's policies, disagreements arose between Kirkpatrick and the administration, aggravated by her perception of sexual discrimination within the government. She resigned in 1985 and returned to teaching at Georgetown University. She remains in the public eye through her articles and appearances at Republican events.

Juanita Morris Kreps (1921–)
United States secretary of commerce

THE FIRST ECONOMIST TO HOLD THE CABINET position of secretary of commerce was also the first woman in the job. Juanita Kreps, who served from 1977 to 1979, had a stellar reputation in her field when President Jimmy Carter appointed her to the post. She had taught at Duke University since 1955 and was made vice-president of the school in 1973. A prolific author, her books included *Sex in the Marketplace: American Women at Work* (1971). She was on the board of directors at Eastman Kodak, J.C. Penney, and other companies, as well as the New York Stock Exchange. Even the beginning of her career was impressive: She had worked for the National War Labor Board during World War II, just after graduating from college.

Kreps believed that the Department of Commerce should be concerned not only with business owners, its traditional focus, but with the needs of workers and consumers. As an economist, she was especially concerned with examining and improving the position of older people and women in the workforce, believing that their roles were important and often overlooked.

Nadezhda Konstantinovna Krupskaya (1869–1939)
Russian Communist party leader, revolutionary

NADEZHDA KRUPSKAYA MAY BE KNOWN BEST AS the wife of Vladimir Lenin, the leader of the revolution that transformed Russia into the Soviet Union, but she was an active revolutionary in her own right. She was working as a geography teacher in St. Petersburg when she met Lenin in 1893. Already a believer in Marxism, she threw herself into revolutionary activities as his partner. In 1896 she

Vladimir Lenin and Nadezhda Krupskaya

was sentenced to exile for her role in a workers' strike, and she asked to be sent to Shushenskoye, Siberia. There she was able to join and marry Lenin, who was also in exile. After they were released, Krupskaya helped her husband carry out underground activities throughout Europe, serving as his personal secretary and editing newspapers.

In early 1917 Krupskaya returned to Russia, where she spread Lenin's message of change in preparation for his seizure of power in October of that year. Krupskaya played important roles within the Communist government, including developing the party's education program. She continued to hold political posts after Lenin's death in 1924, although she disagreed with his successor, Joseph Stalin, and lost much of her influence.

Madeleine May Kunin (1933–)
Governor of Vermont, ambassador to Switzerland

MADELEINE MAY WAS SIX YEARS OLD WHEN HER mother, determined to keep her two children safe from the Nazis, fled Zurich, Switzerland, and came to America. Growing up in New York and Massachusetts, Madeleine didn't plan to be a politician. She earned a journalism degree from Columbia University; moved to Burlington, Vermont; and married Dr. Arthur Kunin. They had four children.

In 1970 she visited Switzerland and witnessed the struggle of Swiss women to gain the vote. It inspired her to enter politics.

Running on a platform of protection for the environment, children, and the poor, Kunin was elected to the Vermont House of Representatives in 1973, then she served two terms as lieutenant governor. In 1984 she became Vermont's first woman and first Jewish governor. While she was in office, Kunin eliminated the budget deficit, raised money for education, and enacted new environmental laws despite opposition from the influential ski industry. She made a point of soliciting opinions from advisers on all sides. Critics called this "wishy-washy," but supporters reelected her twice before she announced she would not run again.

In 1993 President Bill Clinton appointed Kunin deputy secretary of education. Three years later, he made her ambassador to Switzerland, and she returned to her native country once again.

Lakshmi Bai (1830?–1858)
Rani of Jhansi

BORN INTO A HIGH-CASTE HINDU FAMILY, LAKSHMI Bai married the maharaja of Jhansi, a small kingdom in northern India. She had spent her childhood studying, riding, and playing with her brothers, so she felt confined in her decorous role as maharani (commonly shortened to rani). When her husband died in 1853, Lakshmi planned to serve as regent for their adopted son, Damodar Rao, who was not yet old enough to rule. However, the British, seeing a chance to take over, rejected the succession. After lengthy battles in court, Lakshmi was deposed.

By 1857 much of India was in open rebellion, and the British asked Lakshmi to restore order in Jhansi on their behalf. Once she had taken control, though, she wasn't about to give it up. She trained an army and organized women to help strengthen the capital city's defenses. When the British attacked, she led the way into battle, dressed as a man, wielding a sword in each hand, and guiding her horse by holding the reins in her teeth. In spite of all, Jhansi was captured. Lakshmi escaped but was killed in a battle the following year, becoming a martyr in the Indian war for independence.

Bertha Knight Landes (1868–1943)
Mayor of Seattle

BERTHA LANDES MOVED TO SEATTLE, WASHINGTON, in 1895 when her husband, Henry, was hired at the university there. A member of an old New England family, she was from Massachusetts and was college-educated, having graduated from Indiana University in 1891. Landes began running social service clubs for women, slapping her rough new hometown into shape.

In 1922 Landes was elected to the city council and, during her second term, became its president. As such, she stood in for Mayor Edwin "Doc" Brown when he was out of town in 1924. She took this opportunity to mount a crusade against the city's notorious problems with gambling and vice, even firing the chief of police. The mayor rushed home and returned things to normal, but Landes had impressed people. She defeated Doc Brown in the 1926 election, becoming the first female mayor of a major American city.

As mayor, Landes tried to expand the park system and supported public utilities. But her term was only two years long. The newspapers and unions supported her in 1928, but Seattle had had enough of the high-minded approach, and Landes was defeated.

troops intervened. Eventually a group led by Sanford B. Dole forced her to abdicate.

Despite opposition from the natives and their former queen, Hawaii was annexed by the United States in 1898. From then until her death, Liliuokalani, strong-willed and beloved by her people, devoted herself to traditional culture, especially music. She is the composer of the song "Aloha Oe."

Liliuokalani (1838–1917)
Queen of Hawaii

TO NATIVE HAWAIIANS, LILIUOKALANI, THE LAST royal ruler of the islands, is a symbol of a time when a sacred bond existed between the people and their land, and Hawaii was ruled by Hawaiians. In 1874 Liliuokalani's brother succeeded to the throne and, during his reign, allowed a cabinet of American administrators to take over many of his ruling powers. A constitution passed by that cabinet gave voting rights to foreign residents that were not also granted to the natives.

When Liliuokalani ascended the throne in 1891—the first woman to do so—she attempted to regain control of the islands. But the United States, which had many commercial privileges as well as a naval base at Pearl Harbor, was reluctant to give up its power. When Liliuokalani attempted to set up a new cabinet and constitution in 1893, American

Livia Drusilla (58 B.C.E.–29 C.E.)
Roman empress

LIVIA DRUSILLA, LATER KNOWN AS LIVIA AUGUSTA or Julia Augusta, achieved all the power that her great ambition could desire through her marriage to the Roman emperor Augustus. However, she was sadly disappointed by his successor, her son Tiberius. To the Roman people, she was a symbol of the virtuous, dutiful wife, but the private Livia was an unscrupulous schemer.

Livia and Augustus were devoted to each other. He relied on her advice and made her second-in-command of the vast Roman Empire. But Tiberius, born during Livia's first marriage, hated his stepfather and resisted all efforts to inspire his obedience and love. Livia's greatest wish was to see Tiberius succeed Augustus, and she may indeed have conspired against Augustus' descendants from his first marriage, who came before Tiberius in line for the throne.

Livia finally got Tiberius to behave and, when Augustus died in 14 C.E., made sure Tiberius was in control before announcing Augustus' death. After all her hard work, she spent the rest of her life struggling with Tiberius, who resented her influence with the people and wouldn't let her rule with him, as she had with Augustus.

Clare Boothe Luce (1903–1987)
Public official, writer

I**T'S NOT EASY TO FIT** C**LARE** B**OOTHE** L**UCE**, **ONE** of the most influential women of her day, into one category. She was a politician, but she was also a playwright, journalist, editor, the wife of Henry Luce (the publisher of *Time*, *Life*, and *Fortune* magazines), and even, briefly in her youth, an actress.

In the early 1930s, Luce was an editorial assistant at *Vogue* magazine, then managing editor at *Vanity Fair*. After World War II began in Europe, she wrote about the conflict for *Life*. She visited Africa and Asia, always attempting to visit the battlefront and interviewing important people, such as Chiang Kai-shek and his wife, Soong Mei-ling. She published fiction and satirical sketches. Her plays were produced on Broadway, and some were made into films, most notably her satire, *The Women*.

Luce's career in politics began in 1940, when she campaigned for the Republican presidential candidate, Wendell Willkie, who lost to Franklin D. Roosevelt. In 1942 she was elected to the first of her two terms in the House of Representatives, where she became known for coining phrases and for her opposition to the Democratic administration. She served three years as ambassador to Italy during President Dwight Eisenhower's administration. After that, although she occasionally returned to the public eye, she was mostly retired. In 1983, in recognition of Luce's exceptional and wide-ranging contributions to the country, Ronald Reagan awarded her the Presidential Medal of Freedom, one of America's highest honors.

Dame Enid Muriel Lyons (1897–1981)
Member of the Australian parliament, cabinet minister

T**HE MARRIAGE OF** E**NID** B**URNELL AND** J**OSEPH** A. Lyons in 1915 was both a personal and a political partnership. He was already the Tasmanian minister for education. She was just 18 years old, and she had converted to Catholicism for his sake. Joseph rose to the position of Australian prime minister, which he held from 1932 until his death in

> "I believe, very sincerely, that any woman entering the public arena must be prepared to work as men work; . . . But because I am a woman, and cannot divest myself of those qualities that are inherent in my sex, and because every one of us speaks broadly in terms of his own experience, Honourable Members will have to become accustomed to the application of the homely metaphor of the kitchen rather than those of the operating theatre, the workshop, or the farm. They must also become accustomed to the application to all kinds of measures of the touchstone of their effect upon home and family life."
>
> E**NID** L**YONS**
> **Maiden speech in Parliament**

1939. Throughout his career, Enid was his closest adviser, to such an extent that he considered his accomplishments to be equally hers. Even while caring for their 12 children, she was constantly at his side and often used her own skills as a public speaker to support the moderate policies of his United Australia party.

After her husband's death, Enid was offered Joseph's seat in Parliament. Instead, she campaigned for a different district seat in 1943 and won. She served her Tasmanian constituents well, involving herself in legislation about shipping, agriculture, mining, and family issues. With her appointment in 1949 as vice-president of the Executive Council, she became Australia's first female cabinet minister. Illness forced her to resign in 1951, but she remained active as an author, newspaper columnist, and member of the national radio service board.

Wilma Mankiller (1945–)
Chief of the Cherokee Nation

Wilma Mankiller, born to a full-blood Cherokee father and a Dutch mother, was just a girl when her family was relocated from their farm in Oklahoma to San Francisco by the Bureau of Indian Affairs. Mankiller adapted to life in the city. She married after high school, had two children, and became a homemaker. Then, in 1969, a group of Indians occupied Alcatraz Island off San Francisco, claiming the land was their tribal heritage. Mankiller supported their stand and grew interested in other Native American causes as well.

Mankiller decided to go to college, then returned to Oklahoma in 1977 to reclaim her grandfather's land. She worked as economic coordinator for the Cherokee tribe, creating community development programs that became national models. In 1985 she became the first woman to lead a Native American tribe when she took over for the chief, Ross Swimmer, who had accepted a job in Washington, D.C. She was elected to the position two years later.

As chief, Mankiller was an effective spokesperson, who increased national awareness of the problems faced by the Cherokees. She established programs that improved the tribe's economy and education while preserving their native language

and culture. During her time in office, Mankiller suffered the continuing complications of a terrible car accident she experienced in 1979, as well as muscular dystrophy. She retired in 1994.

Margaret (1353–1412)
Queen of Denmark, Norway, and Sweden

As was the custom, Princess Margaret of Denmark married King Haakon VI of Norway when she was just a girl. She became active in medieval European politics after the death of her father, King Valdemar IV in 1376. Margaret used charm and diplomacy to maneuver her six-year-old son, Olaf, onto the Danish throne, with herself as regent. Haakon died five years later, and Olaf inherited the Norwegian throne, bringing that country under Margaret's control as well. Upon Olaf's death in 1387, Margaret was proclaimed queen in her own right.

Nobles from neighboring Sweden asked Margaret to help them overthrow their unpopular king, Albrecht. This was done, and she was crowned queen of Sweden in 1388. Thus, all three Scandinavian kingdoms came together under one monarch. Margaret's nephew, Erik, was designated king of this so-called Kalmar Union in 1397, but she remained the acknowledged ruler until her death.

Margaret kept her domain secure and intact, a task both difficult and expensive. She made many enemies among her subjects for the heavy taxes she imposed. But the Kalmar Union endured until 1523, over a century after her death.

Maria Theresa (1717–1780)
Ruler of the Hapsburg Empire

In 1740, the year Maria Theresa's father died and she took control of the Hapsburg Empire, Frederick II the Great of Prussia invaded, determined to annex one of her most profitable holdings, Silesia, in what is now Poland. Her attempts to regain the lost province involved her in other wars, too, including the Seven Years' War, which lasted from 1756 to 1763. During these conflicts her empire—spanning Austria, Hungary, and many other Central European lands—changed shape as territory was lost and won, and people of many different religions struggled to get along.

Although she failed in her attempts to recapture Silesia, Maria Theresa accomplished much during her reign. She had inherited a debt-ridden monarchy, an inefficient government, weak army, and unhappy subjects. But she was intelligent, practical, and able to recognize good advice when she heard it. During her reign, she reorganized the central government, revitalized the economy, reformed education at all levels, and granted more freedom to the peasants. She was an ardent Catholic; some religious persecutions did take place at her command. Over all, however, she worked toward separating church from state and allowed certain religious freedoms. Devoted to her husband, Francis, she bore him 16 children, one of whom was the infamous Marie-Antoinette, wife of the French King Louis XVI. According to law Francis was the emperor, but she was known to be the true power behind the crown.

Mary I (1516–1558)
Queen of England

Known to posterity as "Bloody Mary," the first English queen to rule in her own right lived a life of disappointment. Her father, Henry VIII, divorced her mother, Catherine of Aragon. Bitterly resenting such treatment of her beloved mother and the fact that he had severed ties with her equally beloved Roman Catholic church, Mary watched as four more wives arrived and vanished, either by divorce or execution. Through it all, she remained a devout Catholic.

Mary survived her father and her brother, Edward VI, and ascended the throne in 1553, at age 37. She immediately restored ties with Rome and married the Catholic Philip of Spain. This upset her English subjects, many of whom despised the Spanish and feared losing property and privileges they had taken from Catholics with Henry's approval. In fact, they had good reason to worry: Mary restored laws that called for Protestants to be executed as heretics. Hundreds of Protestants were burned at the stake, and smoke from those fires blackened Mary's name. She ruled well in other ways but is remembered for the horrors resulting from her blind devotion to her faith.

In addition to political and religious worries, Mary's marriage was unsuccessful. Philip returned to Spain when his father died in 1555. He only visited Mary once again, to gain her support in his disastrous war against France, in which England lost Calais. Within months Mary died, knowing that her final failure would be her succession by her Protestant sister Elizabeth.

Mary (1542–1587)
Queen of Scots

Mary, the only daughter of King James V of Scotland, was born into controversy and made things even worse through her own mistakes. Henry VIII of England, who hoped to join England and Scotland, wanted her to marry his son, Edward. Instead Mary's mother engaged her to the heir to the French throne. So in 1548, at age five, Mary went to the French court. She married, reigned, was widowed, and returned to Scotland by the time she was 18. Although true to her Catholic faith, she made a good first impression, promising not to interfere in

her subjects' Protestant religion and attempting to reconcile the bitter religious rivalry.

Despite this positive start, she angered her advisers by marrying Henry, Lord Darnley. He was foolish, an ambitious scoundrel—and a murderer. By the time their son was born, Mary yearned to be rid of her husband. In 1567 her wish came true when Darnley was murdered in mysterious circumstances. She may not have been involved, but she married one of the known conspirators, which made her look guilty. Under pressure, she abdicated in favor of her infant son. Then she made her biggest mistake: she sought sanctuary with Queen Elizabeth in England.

Elizabeth, faced with this unwelcome guest who was too dangerous to either aid or destroy, kept Mary under house arrest for 18 years. Desperate for freedom, Mary became involved in Catholic attempts to depose Elizabeth. In 1587 Mary was found guilty of attempted assassination and was beheaded. Her son eventually succeeded Elizabeth as James I, achieving Henry's aim of uniting England and Scotland.

Masako (1963–)
Crown princess of Japan

MASAKO IS THE DAUGHTER OF JAPAN'S HIGHLY placed vice-minister of foreign affairs, Osawa Hisashi, but she has established her professional credentials on her own merit. An accomplished diplomat, she was educated at Harvard, Tokyo, and Oxford universities, where she specialized in international trade and legal affairs. Her career was exceptionally promising, but in 1993 she left it and married the Japanese crown prince, Naruhito.

Masako and Naruhito met in 1986, and he made it clear right away that he was interested in her. But Masako enjoyed her freedom as a modern woman. She wasn't sure she wanted to become part of the ancient imperial system. At last, in 1992, she accepted his proposals and committed herself to a different sort of diplomatic career, a life of ceremonial rituals, walking a few steps behind her husband, and only voicing opinions approved by the Imperial Household Agency. Ultra-conservatives grumbled that she was too assertive; she expressed her opinions and even laughed in public without covering her mouth. To the people, however—many of whom hope she can bring a human side to the monarchy—she is a role model, and they eagerly wait to see what she will accomplish.

Matilda (1046–1115)
Countess of Tuscany

MATILDA OF TUSCANY RULED A LARGE DOMAIN in northern Italy—not a typical role for a medieval woman. Under the influence of her equally strong and intelligent mother, Beatrice, she studied a variety of subjects. Although it was unusual for a woman to understand political and religious conflicts, she not only understood but played an active part.

Matilda devoted much of her money and power to the Catholic church and, as a result, she had great influence with the popes of her time. During the 1070s Pope Gregory VII engaged in a bitter struggle with the German emperor, Henry IV, who sought to control religious appointments. In 1076 the pope excommunicated Henry. Having lost support, he traveled to Matilda's castle in Canossa and waited for three days in the snow before the pope, Matilda's honored guest, agreed to negotiate with him. She served as mediator, but the episode did not end her troubles with Henry. She continued to defend her lands from his invasions, with only partial success. Toward the end of her life, she devoted herself to spiritual contemplation.

Golda Meir (1898–1978)
Prime minister of Israel

W HEN GOLDA MEIR WAS BORN, THE STATE OF Israel did not yet exist—Meir would help to create and sustain it, becoming the nation's first woman prime minister. She was born Golda Mabovitch in Kiev, Ukraine. But the Jewish community there came under frequent attack, so the family immigrated to the United States, where they struggled to make a living. Golda became an active member of the labor movement and an ardent Zionist, a supporter of the establishment of a Jewish state.

In 1917, the year Golda married Morris Meyerson, Palestine was designated the longed-for homeland. The couple settled there in 1921 and worked on a kibbutz, or collective farm, before taking jobs with the Labor Federation. Golda became increasingly involved in politics, winning support for the cause of an Israeli state separate from Palestine with her eloquent speeches. World War II ended, and in 1948 the state of Israel was born. She took the Hebrew surname, Meir, and served the newborn nation as a member of parliament, minister of labor, delegate to the United Nations, and, in 1969, as prime minister.

The job of leading Israel, beset on all sides by hostile Arab nations, was a difficult one, but Meir handled it with strength, vision, and warm good humor. Despite the challenges, she was popular with the people and considered an effective world leader by her peers. However, when Egyptian and Syrian forces attacked Israel on the Yom Kippur holiday in 1973, she was criticized for having failed to prepare her military. She resigned the following year but remained an influential public figure until her death from cancer.

Perle Skirvin Mesta (1889–1975)
Political hostess, ambassador

T HE ORIGINAL "HOSTESS WITH THE MOSTES'"— and the inspiration for Irving Berlin's musical *Call Me Madam*—Perle Mesta became a famous political figure by throwing parties. The daughter and wife of rich men, her status, as well as her warmth and charm, enabled her to meet many influential people.

Mesta was introduced to Washington political society when her husband, George, was a consultant to the government during World War I. In the mid-1930s, Mesta, by then a widow, joined the National Woman's party and began working actively in local and national politics. An ardent feminist, she supported the Equal Rights Amendment. She met Senator Harry S. Truman in 1942 and lent her influential presence to his presidential campaign. Her legendary parties raised funds and drew attention to her candidate. Her friendship with the Truman family would last, and her career as a hostess paralleled his progress as a politician. After Truman's victory Mesta continued to preside over White House events, since the first lady didn't enjoy that role.

Truman appointed Mesta minister to Luxembourg in 1949 (her full title was Envoy Extraordinary and Minister Plenipotentiary), not because of her party-giving, but for her shrewd common sense. She had successfully managed oil, real estate, and machine businesses inherited from her father and husband. She considered her diplomatic appointment a victory for women who had been demanding more such posts.

Patsy Takemoto Mink (1927–)
United States congresswoman

PATSY TAKEMOTO WAS A TEENAGER IN MAUI, Hawaii, when World War II broke out. It was a time when American-born people of Japanese heritage, like Patsy, suffered terrible discrimination. Many had never even visited their parents' homeland, but Japan was an enemy in the conflict, and this was enough to cause them to be persecuted. The experience inspired Patsy to make a career of challenging powerful institutions in defense of the underdog.

In 1951 she earned her law degree from the University of Chicago and married John Mink, a geophysicist of German descent. Her sex and her interracial marriage proved to be obstacles to finding a job, so she opened her own practice. She also became active in Democratic politics. In 1956 Mink was elected to the Hawaii House of Representatives; the 1958 elections took her to the state Senate; and in 1964 her bid for the United States House of Representatives was successful.

The first Japanese American congresswoman, she has served eight terms so far, taking time during the 1980s to return to Hawaiian politics.

In Congress Mink spoke out against the Vietnam War and emphasized the importance of domestic issues, such as education and health care. She has maintained her liberal point of view, even as Congress has become more conservative.

Esther Hobart Morris (1814–1902)
Justice of the peace, suffragist

IT WAS HARD TO SAY "NO" TO ESTHER MORRIS. HER forceful character and impressive stature—she was six feet tall (1.8 m) and weighed almost 200 pounds (91 kg)—worked to her advantage in her roles as a women's suffrage leader and justice of the peace. One person who didn't disagree with her was William H. Bright, the first legislator elected in Wyoming Territory. Morris is said to have urged him to introduce a bill for women's suffrage. The bill passed in 1869, 50 years before national suffrage became a reality.

The next year, Morris became the first woman appointed justice of the peace, in charge of keeping order in South Pass City, a town populated with gold miners. During her nine months in office, she tried over 70 cases. Her decisions were quickly reached but solid; none were ever reversed. She left the job when her marriage broke up, but not before she had the satisfaction of ruling against her own husband for having assaulted her. In today's legal system it wouldn't be possible for a judge to preside in a case that involved her. But those were the early days of law and order, and she was living in the "wild" West. Hobart went on to devote herself to reform, earning a reputation for being Wyoming's "mother" of women's suffrage.

Carol Moseley-Braun (1947–)
United States congresswoman

CAROL MOSELEY-BRAUN, A DIVORCED, SINGLE mother from a working-class background, overcame odds to become the country's first black female senator in 1992. After her triumph she acknowledged being a "symbol of hope and change" but stated that she intended to be hardworking and effective, too.

Moseley-Braun was born, raised, and educated in Chicago. She received her law degree from the University of Chicago in 1972 and went on to serve as assistant United States attorney, Illinois state representative, and county executive. Outrage over the Senate's handling of the Anita Hill hearings in 1991 inspired her to challenge what she saw as an exclusive club of white, rich men. Running for the Senate without funding or support from other politicians, she was given little chance of winning. Her image was also tarnished by accusations of hiring favorites and mishandling money, setbacks she handled with composure. She remained dedicated to her causes: the rights of minorities and women, and the welfare of the inner-city poor. Her surprise victory was the result of support from a wide range of voters, across racial and economic boundaries.

Belle Lindner Moskowitz (1877–1933)
Political adviser

ALTHOUGH NOT AN ELECTED POLITICIAN, BELLE Moskowitz had great political influence as the adviser of New York's governor, Alfred E. Smith. She was a pioneer in the field of public relations, a new concept in the 1920s. An energetic, forceful person with a strong social conscience, Moskowitz began her career as a welfare worker, with a special interest in urban problems and the plight of working women. Her interest in social reforms, such as women's rights, public aid for the poor, support of labor unions, and defense of free speech, led to an involvement in politics. At first, Moskowitz campaigned for Progressive party candidates, but she eventually decided that an established party could accomplish her goals more effectively.

Moskowitz's career really took off in 1918, when she met Alfred E. Smith, the Democratic candidate for governor. Women had just been granted the right to vote in New York State, and Moskowitz suggested a campaign aimed especially at this new group of voters. It was a great success, and, once in office, Smith continued to seek her opinions. In her unofficial but important position, Moskowitz gathered

information and acted as a link with other politicians. She tried long and hard to help her friend Smith get elected president but, to her regret, she never succeeded.

Constance Baker Motley (1921–)
Federal judge, state senator

CONSTANCE BAKER MOTLEY, ONE OF 12 CHILDREN, grew up in New Haven, Connecticut. As a high school student, she joined the NAACP and decided that she wanted to be a lawyer, but money was always scarce. Then, when she was 18, the white philanthropist Clarence Blakeslee heard Motley deliver an impassioned speech about civil rights and was so impressed that he decided to fund her education.

Motley was still in law school at Columbia University when she began working for Thurgood Marshall at the NAACP Legal Defense and Educational Fund. She remained with the association for ten years and was involved in most of the crucial civil rights cases of the day. One of her most famous victories occurred in 1962, when she represented James Meredith, an African American seeking the right to attend the all-white University of Mississippi.

In 1964 she began a series of rapid-fire, groundbreaking political accomplishments, becoming the first black woman to win a seat in the New York State Senate. The next year, she was the first African American and the first woman to be elected Manhattan borough president. And the year after that, she became the country's first black female federal judge when she was appointed to the United States District Court for the Southern District of New York. She continues to serve in the District Court, where since 1986, she has been the senior judge.

Bess Myerson (1924–)
Public official, journalist

BORN IN THE BRONX, NEW YORK, TO RUSSIAN immigrants, Bess Myerson received national attention when she became the first Jewish woman to win the Miss America Pageant in 1945. She attracted even more notice when she resigned from the

pageant's publicity tour to protest the anti-Semitism she had experienced there.

Myerson became an award-winning reporter, writing investigative newspaper articles and books on consumer protection, as well as producing radio and television documentaries. From 1969 to 1973, she served as commissioner of New York City's Department of Consumer Affairs. She used her balanced perspective and ability to reconcile diverse interests to pass legislative reforms. She helped write the Consumer Protection Act, addressing such issues as false advertising; it inspired similar laws in many other cities. Later Myerson turned her attention to campaigning for the arts, serving as commissioner for the New York Department of Cultural Affairs from 1982 to 1987. Most recently, she has made a point of supporting Jewish causes, such as the Anti-Defamation League.

Alva Reimer Myrdal (1902–1986)
Swedish ambassador, government official, scholar

Alva Reimer married Gunnar Myrdal in 1924, the year she graduated from the University of Stockholm. In the following years, they traveled extensively, and Alva pursued studies in economics, psychology, and philosophy. Together they investigated population problems and economic conditions, and their findings influenced programs adopted by Sweden during the 1930s.

Soon they were internationally renowned, both as a team and separately. In 1949 Alva became director of the Department of Social Affairs of the United Nations in New York City. Two years later she moved to Paris as director of the Department of Social Sciences of UNESCO.

As a politician, Alva Myrdal became involved in many issues: housing, population, child welfare, vocational training for the handicapped, the role of working women, the plight of refugees, and international relations. She became most famous for promoting world disarmament. After serving as Sweden's ambassador to India during the 1950s, she was elected to Parliament in 1962. She led her country's delegation at the disarmament conference in Geneva for many years. Her books include *The Game of Disarmament: How the United States and Russia Run the Arms Race* (1976). She was awarded the Albert Einstein Peace Prize in 1980 and was a corecipient of the Nobel Peace Prize in 1982.

Nguyen Thi Binh (1927–)
Vice-president of Vietnam

Known as "the Flower and Fire" of the Vietnamese revolution, Nguyen Thi Binh used her skills as a diplomat to seek peace for her war-torn homeland. Nguyen's family opposed the

French occupation of their country and the presence of American military support. In 1950 she organized the first anti-American demonstration in Saigon. Her activities caused her to be imprisoned by the French authorities from 1951 to 1954, the year the Geneva peace accord divided Vietnam into North and South zones. Fighting soon broke out between North Vietnam and the foreign-backed government in the South, and the violence escalated into war.

Nguyen became a leader in the National Liberation Front, which wanted the foreign powers to let Vietnam make its own decisions about who would be in charge. She led a delegation to the Paris Peace Conference in 1968, and at last, in 1973, signed the agreement that ended the war. The country was reunified into the Socialist Republic of Vietnam in 1976. Nguyen has since served as minister of education and on the Council of State. Since 1992 she has been vice-president.

Eleanor Holmes Norton (1937–)
United States congresswoman, lawyer

THROUGHOUT HER CAREER ELEANOR NORTON HAS opposed all forms of discrimination. As a lawyer, she defended everyone, from civil rights activists to white supremacists, because she believed in the importance of free speech as granted by the First Amendment. In her own words, she is "against racism and sexism because they are wrong, not because one is black or one is female."

In 1965, immediately after she graduated from Yale Law School, Norton moved to New York City to work for the American Civil Liberties Union. Specializing in First Amendment lawsuits, she won cases involving discrimination against women in the workplace, opposed racially segregated neighborhoods, and campaigned to increase the number of minority employees in city offices and schools. Five years later, Norton became chairperson of the New York City Commission on Human Rights, and in 1973 she founded the National Black Feminist Organization.

Norton broadened the range of her influence from one city to the entire country in 1977, when President Jimmy Carter appointed her to lead the Equal Employment Opportunity Commission, a federal agency in Washington, D.C. Appropriately enough, she was the first chair*woman* of that committee. In 1990 she was elected to serve as the District of Columbia's delegate to the House of Representatives, an office she still holds.

Nur Jahan (1577–1646)
Moghul empress

IN 1611 EMPEROR JAHANGIR, A MEMBER OF THE Moghul dynasty that ruled India for centuries, fell in love with a 40-year-old servant named Mehrunissa. Eventually, he renamed her Nur Jahan—"light of the world"—and she became his favorite wife, on whom he depended completely, saddled as he was with illness, alcoholism, and opium addiction.

For 16 years Nur Jahan ruled the empire through her weak husband. A patron of the arts and a skilled businesswoman, she made the court more splendid than ever. She obeyed the Islamic rule of purdah, which forbade women to be seen outside the harem: during tiger hunts, she rode in a curtained box carried by an elephant.

Unfortunately, Nur Jahan also divided the court into factions, promoting family members to high positions, and changing her allegiances to her husband's children. The emperor's son Khurram rebelled, sparking civil wars. Nur Jahan led her troops into battle, riding her trusty elephant and armed with a bow and arrow. Khurram inherited the throne in 1627 and ruled as Shah

Moghul India

The Moghul empire flourished for less than two centuries—from Babur's capture of Delhi in 1526 to the death of the last true Moghul emperor, Aurangzeb, in 1707. But this was long enough to make a strong mark on Indian culture. The Moghuls were Muslim princes who migrated to northern India from Persia. They built lavish palace fortresses, mosques, and tombs, making liberal use of rose-colored stone and inlaid marble. The most famous example of their architecture is the Taj Mahal in Agra, a tomb built by Shah Jahan to honor his favorite wife, Mumtaz Mahal. The Moghuls were also known for their cultured tolerance, even enthusiastic support of, local customs, arts, and religions.

Jahan. In spite of all the trouble Nur Jahan had caused him, he granted her a generous pension. She was able to enjoy a luxurious retirement during her last years.

Nzinga Mbandi (approximately 1580–1663)
Queen of the Mbundu

THE PORTUGUESE, IN THEIR EFFORTS TO COLONIZE Africa and establish a slave trade, attempted to conquer and convert the Mbundu people of Ndongo (now Angola) for over a century. When they finally succeeded in 1618, Nzinga Mbandi saw an opportunity to seize control from her brother, the tribe's ruler. She allowed the Portuguese to baptize her as a Catholic and attempted to collaborate with them. These efforts failed, but she did become queen after her brother and his son died in 1624.

Nzinga's dealings with the European invaders continued to be difficult. She used both diplomacy and acts of barbarity to influence them—and found that barbarity usually worked better. Armed to the teeth, she led both male and female warriors in violent attacks on her enemies. The Portuguese tried to install their own ruler of the Mbundu, but the people ignored this puppet chief. To increase her power, Nzinga made alliances with some neighboring kingdoms and conquered others. During the 1640s, she aligned herself with the Dutch, Portugal's rivals, and built profitable slave-trading centers. At last, in 1656, she concluded a fairly stable peace with the Portuguese and ruled in partnership with them.

Sandra Day O'Connor (1930–)
United States Supreme Court justice

SANDRA DAY O'CONNOR GREW UP ON A LARGE ranch in Arizona near the New Mexico border. It took her only five years to earn both an undergraduate degree and a law degree from Stanford University in California. However, after leaving school in 1952, the only job offer she received from a private law firm was as a legal secretary. Undaunted, she pursued public positions, working as a deputy county attorney and civilian army lawyer. Returning to Arizona with her husband, John, she became assistant attorney general in 1965. O'Connor was also involved in community and Republican-party activities. As a result, she was selected to fill a vacancy in the state Senate in 1969, then elected to two full terms, during the last of which she served as majority leader. Election as a trial judge and appointment to the Arizona Court of Appeals followed.

In 1981 O'Connor broke new ground when President Ronald Reagan made her the first woman justice on the United States Supreme Court. As a rule, O'Connor has voted conservatively, but she has also given support to women's rights—and has kept everyone on their toes with occasional swings to the liberal side.

Ertha Pascal-Trouillot (1943–)

Provisional president of Haiti,
Supreme Court justice

SINCE 1957, WHEN FRANÇOIS DUVALIER CAME TO power, Haiti has suffered under many dictators who terrorized the citizens and left the economy in tatters. For a brief time, from 1990 to 1991, Haitians' hopes were raised as Ertha Pascal-Trouillot took the office of provisional president, holding the fort until the first truly democratic elections could be held. Elegant and intelligent, Pascal-Trouillot was a lawyer. She had been the first woman appointed to the Haitian Supreme Court in 1986 and had worked on revisions of the civil and penal codes. However, although she came from a poor family, she had made her way into the elite society of a poverty-stricken nation, and her ties to the Duvalier regime were under suspicion.

The people triumphantly elected Jean-Bertrand Aristide, a priest who promised to end corruption, in December 1990. In a dramatic turn of events for Pascal-Trouillot, a former Duvalier henchman named Roger Lafontant took her hostage, proclaiming himself president and holding her for 12 hours before he was arrested. After Aristide's inauguration in February, Pascal-Trouillot was placed under house arrest for her supposed association with Duvalier. Released a month later, she retreated from public view. That fall, Aristide was ousted by yet another military coup.

Frances Perkins (1880–1965)

Federal official, social reformer

FRANCES PERKINS WAS THE FIRST WOMAN TO BE appointed to a president's cabinet, and she was involved in many of the social reforms that transformed the United States during the Great Depression.

Throughout her career, she fought to improve the lives of working people by establishing safe working conditions, maximum hours, minimum wages, and unemployment insurance.

Born in Boston, Perkins graduated from Mount Holyoke College and went on to do social work in both Chicago and Philadelphia. In 1910 she accepted a position with the New York City Consumers' League. When the Triangle Shirtwaist Company caught fire in 1911, she witnessed the historic tragedy because she lived nearby. The exits in the sweatshop were blocked, and 146 women workers died. Seeking to change such dreadful conditions, Perkins entered politics. She served in many organizations in New York State, particularly during Governor Al Smith's administration.

Then came the depression of the 1930s, a fearful time for Americans watching the economy spiral downward. In 1932 Franklin D. Roosevelt was elected president. Despite heated opposition to both Perkins's sex and her politics, he named her secretary of labor. She stayed for 12 years, the full length of Roosevelt's term, and she was dramatically effective. Her support was crucial to the passage of such legislation as the Social Security Act of 1935. During World War II, Perkins helped create the character "Rosie the Riveter," a symbol of women working in war industries, and paved the way for greater acceptance of women in the workplace. After leaving the cabinet in 1945, she lectured about labor and industrial problems.

Eva Duarte de Perón (1919–1952)
First lady of Argentina

THE STORY OF EVA PERÓN, KNOWN AS EVITA, IS AS dramatic as she was: She rose from poverty to establish a career as a successful actress, and then went on to become the influential, controversial wife of the president of Argentina.

When Evita met Colonel Juan Domingo Perón in 1944, he was part of the military regime that ran Argentina. They married the following year, and she directed him in a new role, that of an advocate of the underprivileged, an opponent of government corruption. Evita used her skills as an actress to deliver stirring speeches during her husband's presidential campaign. In her elegant clothes, she presented herself as a symbol of what a poor person could become. Juan won the presidency with ease and shared his power with the wife who helped him achieve it.

Evita improved the life of her people, supporting reforms, providing for the needy, and lobbying for women's rights. But behind the righteous facade, she skimmed funds from charitable organizations, censored the press, suppressed opposition through fear and intimidation, and always put her political ambition first.

In 1951, although she had the support of the Argentinian people, the military put an end to Evita's bid for the vice-presidency. She suffered what seemed to be a nervous collapse, but it was soon discovered that she had cancer. Two months after her husband was reelected, Evita died. Without his wife's charisma to sustain his power, Perón was ousted from the presidency.

Isabel Perón (1931–)
President of Argentina

ISABEL PERÓN, THE THIRD WIFE OF JUAN PERÓN, achieved something Juan's former wife, Evita, never did: She became vice-president and then president of Argentina, and she was the first woman to hold those offices. Isabel never attempted to replace Evita. Instead, she used the people's reverence for their dead heroine as a rallying point for her husband's followers.

When they met in 1961, Juan Perón was a deposed dictator in exile and Isabel was a professional dancer. Because Juan could not enter Argentina, his new wife gradually assumed the role of go-between. She campaigned, negotiated, and tried to unify the opposing factions of the political party he still controlled.

In 1972 Juan returned to Argentina and ran again for president. His announcement that Isabel would be his vice-presidential candidate was met with surprise and anger, but he won the election. Poor health soon forced him to turn control over to Isabel, and in 1974 he died. As president, Isabel faced daunting challenges. Argentina was ravaged by violence and economic instability, and the politically inexperienced Isabel could not rely on a charismatic personality, like Juan or Evita. She was arrested during a military coup in 1976 and endured imprisonment and exile in Spain before returning to her homeland to live as quietly as possible.

Esther Eggertsen Peterson (1906–1997)
Assistant secretary of labor, presidential adviser

ESTHER EGGERTSEN, A NATIVE OF PROVO, UTAH, was studying physical education at Columbia University in New York City when her future husband, Oliver Peterson, changed her interests by explaining his work with the labor movement. Not

51

long afterward, in the early 1930s, Esther met a group of Boston dressmakers who were conducting what they called a "heart-break strike" at their factory. They had been ordered to sew a heart-shaped pocket for the same low wage they received for making a much simpler square one. This was the call to action that Esther needed. From then on, she fought to improve conditions for workers and help them get an education. Between 1948 and 1957, Oliver was assigned to posts in Sweden and Belgium, but Esther didn't pause in her campaign. She addressed it on an international level.

Peterson took a job as a lobbyist with the AFL-CIO in 1958, representing labor unions' causes to congressmen in Washington, D.C. In 1961 President John F. Kennedy assigned her to direct the Women's Bureau of the Department of Labor. That position was upgraded to assistant secretary of labor the following year, making her the highest-ranking woman in the federal government at the time. She went on to serve on committees under presidents Johnson, Nixon, Ford, and Carter.

Dorothy Peto (1886–1974)
British police superintendent

DURING WORLD WAR I, WHILE SO MANY MEN were away, Britain allowed women to take on some police duties as volunteers, although the official police forces weren't especially happy about

it. One of the most enthusiastic recruits was Dorothy Peto, who soon became deputy director of the volunteers in Bristol.

As the numbers of women on patrol increased, the authorities had to admit that they were helpful. In 1930 it was decided that an official force was warranted, and the Metropolitan Women's Police was established in London as a branch of Scotland Yard. Peto was brought from Liverpool, where she had been director of women's police patrols since 1927, to be the first superintendent. There were challenges to be overcome, including earning the public's respect and building up the necessary stamina. However, it was soon noticed that the women officers performed observation duties with more resourcefulness and discretion than the men. Peto led the force until her retirement at age 60.

Maria de Lourdes Pintasilgo (1930–)
Prime minister of Portugal

MARIA DE LOURDES PINTASILGO WAS THE FIRST woman prime minister of Portugal, a country troubled by continued political and economic instability. Having gone from being a monarchy to a republic to a dictatorship, and then back to being a republic again, Portugal was a country searching for a way to end the cycle of revolution and resignation. Pintasilgo held the fort in 1979 as a nonpartisan head of a caretaker government. Her term lasted six months, until the next elections were held.

Growing up in Abrantes, Pintasilgo loved writing poetry and playing the piano. She pursued a career in chemical engineering, both to prove that a woman could do it and to learn a skill that would help improve conditions for workers. Although she began a career as a scientific researcher, her interest in international politics and social welfare gradually took precedence. Her many affiliations included work with Graal (a Catholic organization), and UNESCO. During her time as prime minister, she received less satisfaction from passing laws than she did from seeing Portuguese women begin to follow her example and speak up.

Pintasilgo has written extensively on international affairs and the status of women. Her books include *Les nouveaux féminismes* (1980, New feminisms) and *As minhas respostas* (1985, My answer).

Milka Planinc (1924–)
Prime minister of Yugoslavia

YUGOSLAVIA HAS REPEATEDLY BEEN DIVIDED UP, redistributed, and patched back together. It has been ruled by kings, by Adolf Hitler, and by the Communist Josip Broz Tito. For a time, Tito united six historical regions inhabited by 18 ethnic groups who followed three different religions. He was Milka Planinc's hero. By following him, she became the first woman prime minister of a communist country.

Planinc, who was born in Croatia, was 17 years old when the Axis powers seized Yugoslavia during World War II. She eagerly followed the career of Tito, who emerged as the leader of the Communist Partisans, the main movement opposing Axis control. At age 19, Planinc joined the group, enduring many wartime hardships. Afterward, she continued to support Tito while he organized and led a new Yugoslavian government. Joining his Communist party, Planinc worked her way up through administrative committees. Even when other Yugoslavs rebelled against Tito for curbing free speech and civil liberties, she remained devoted.

Her career culminated with her election as prime minister in 1982. She faced the challenges of leading a weak central government in a country plagued by inflation, foreign debts, and ethnic strife. After her term ended in 1986, she remained committed to the party, even when the fragile unity dissolved into civil war and the boundaries of the country were, once again, redrawn.

Biljana Plavsic (1930–)
President of the Serb Republic of Bosnia and Herzegovina

BEFORE TURNING TO POLITICS IN THE 1990s, Biljana Plavsic was a biology professor at Sarajevo University. But, as one of the Serbian minority in Bosnia, she was passionately opposed to her homeland's secession from Yugoslavia in 1992. She gained prominence in the nationalist Serbian Democratic party, and when the Serbs rebelled and established the Republika Srpska (Serb Republic) with Radovan Karadzic as president, Plavsic was one of two vice presidents. Serbs were urged to take up arms against Bosnian Muslims and Croats. The terrible bloodshed that followed was given the comparatively innocent-sounding name, "ethnic cleansing," but it was simply genocide. The ardent Plavsic declared, "There are 12 million Serbs in the former Yugoslavia. We can afford to lose 6 million on the battlefield."

Finally, the international community intervened. In 1995 a peace agreement was negotiated in Dayton, Ohio, that provided for NATO troops to enforce a cease-fire, partitioned the country into two areas, and deposed Karadzic. Plavsic became president of the Serb Republic in 1996 and, changing strategies, accused her ex-boss of corruption. She presented herself as a champion of democracy and expressed a sudden willingness to abide by the Dayton Agreement. Representatives from the West were leery but backed her opposition to Karadzic, who had set up his own government in the southern city of Pale.

Plavsic's moderate stance cost her public support. She lost elections held in 1998 to a radical nationalist, Nikola Poplasen.

Jeanne Antoinette Poisson Le Normant d'Étioles, Marquise de Pompadour (1721–1764)
Mistress of King Louis XV of France

CHARMING, WITTY, AND THE TOAST OF PARISIAN society, the ambitious Jeanne Antoinette Le Normant d'Étioles had almost everything she wanted, and in 1745 her loftiest wishes were granted: Separating from her husband, she began a career as King Louis XV's mistress and was given the title Marquise de Pompadour. She would influence the king's policies to such an extent that she was considered the true ruler of France.

The king was capable of making decisions but so shy that he preferred to have Madame de Pompadour speak for him. He also required a great deal of entertaining, which she supplied in the form of theatrical productions and patronage of the decorative arts. In these areas her tastes reigned supreme. Many landmarks, such as the Place de la Concorde in Paris, were built under her supervision.

Madame de Pompadour was not as talented at politics as she was at the arts, although she tried, encouraging alliances, appointing officials, and

receiving diplomats. She meant well, but her policies led to France's disastrous defeat by England and Prussia in the Seven Years' War of 1756 to 1763. Although Louis took other mistresses, she never lost her position as his closest adviser. She died at the age of 43, leaving a country beset by debts and frustrated with ineffectual government—a prime setting for revolution.

Jeannette Pickering Rankin (1880–1973)

Congresswoman, women's rights activist, pacifist

JEANNETTE RANKIN BELIEVED THAT THE PEACE movement and women's rights issues were inseparable, and she supported both causes throughout her career. She became the first woman ever elected to the House of Representatives in 1916—

> **"You can no more win a war than you can win an earthquake."**
>
> —JEANNETTE RANKIN
> **Quoted in *Jeannette Rankin: First Lady in Congress*, 1941**

before all women in the country were even granted the right to vote. The 19th Amendment, which Rankin herself introduced in Congress, was ratified in 1920.

Rankin grew up on a prosperous farm in Montana, and she possessed the individualism of the frontier. She trained as a social worker but soon decided to approach reform on a larger scale, through politics. Joining the campaign for women's suffrage, she helped women win the vote in her home state and in Washington State.

After her election to Congress, Rankin spoke out against the United States' participation in World War I. Her courageous stand made her unpopular with voters, and she was not reelected until 1940. In the intervening years, she worked with Jane Addams and Florence Kelley to help establish the Women's International League for Peace and Freedom. In 1941, after the Japanese attack on Pearl Harbor, she was the only legislator to vote against America's decision to enter World War II. This time she had to be rescued by the police from an angry mob.

Even out of the public eye, Rankin continued her work. She traveled to India to study the nonviolent tactics of Mohandas Gandhi and opposed the war in Korea. In the 1960s her ideas at last attracted followers. She was 87 when she led the 5,000-woman "Jeannette Rankin Brigade" in a march on Capitol Hill to protest the country's participation in the Vietnam War.

Dixy Lee Ray (1914–1994)

Public official, governor of Washington, zoologist

DIXY LEE RAY SPENT HER CHILDHOOD IN TACOMA, Washington, where she developed a love of the outdoors and an interest in marine life. She earned her Ph.D. at Stanford and became a professor of zoology at Seattle's University of Washington in 1945. While there she joined numerous scientific and government groups. She also became the director of the Pacific Science Center, which she helped turn into a prestigious institution.

Ray's emphasis on encouraging public interest in science led President Richard Nixon to appoint her to the Atomic Energy Commission (AEC) in 1972. The job took her to Washington, D.C., where

she lived in a mobile home custom-built to accommodate her two dogs, a 100-pound (45-kg) Scottish deerhound and a miniature poodle, who frequently accompanied her to work. In 1973 she was named chairperson of the AEC. To some people her appointment seemed contradictory, since she had long been a leading advocate for ecological research. However, Ray considered nuclear power to be a necessary alternative to fossil fuels.

Returning to her beloved Pacific Northwest, Ray was elected governor of Washington State in 1976 and served one term. She remained outspoken to the end of her life. The controversial books she cowrote with Lou Guzzo, *Trashing the Planet* (1990) and *Environmental Overkill* (1993), criticized some environmental activists for failing to educate themselves properly about the issues.

Raziyya (unknown–1240)
Sultana of northern India

ILTUTMISH, A FORMER SLAVE WHO BECAME THE most powerful sultan in northern India, regretfully acknowledged that none of his sons were fit to rule. But his daughter, Raziyya, had a talent for politics and had eagerly trained to lead armies. He named her his heir.

When Iltutmish died in 1236, the nobles refused to let a woman rule. So to preserve peace, she let one of her brothers become sultan. He was so incompetent that the nobles soon asked Raziyya to assume her rightful place. As enlightened as her father had suspected, she supported the arts and education, built roads and wells, and encouraged trade.

But her liberal behavior offended her enemies. Although she was Muslim, she sometimes cast off her veil and wore men's clothes. She held public meetings to discuss state affairs, and extended justice to members of all religions at a time when Muslims and Hindus were locked in bitter conflict.

In 1240 Raziyya was deposed during a coup, then killed on the battlefield while trying to regain her throne. Her tomb became a place of pilgrimage for her devoted subjects.

Janet Reno (1938–)
Attorney general of the United States

WHEN JANET RENO WAS 16 YEARS OLD, HER parents bought property in the Everglades near Miami, Florida. There, Reno's mother, Jane, built the family's new house by herself. Reno was profoundly inspired by her mother's determination and capability. She made a point of applying those same qualities to her own career, and she lived in the house until 1993, when she was appointed the first woman attorney general of the United States.

Reno earned her degree from Harvard Law School in 1963, then returned home to Miami, where she practiced in a small firm. By 1973 she had joined the state attorney's office. Her experiences there convinced her of the importance of changing the conditions that lead to crime rather than just punishing criminals. After her appointment in 1978 as Florida's first female state attorney, she implemented many innovative programs, including counseling, treatment, and community self-policing.

Since becoming attorney general, Reno has handled many difficult issues, including pressure to authorize legal investigations of President Bill Clinton and other top officials. Politicians often disagree with her decisions, but few would question her reputation as a hard worker and a thorough, independent-minded thinker.

Ann Willis Richards (1933–)
Governor of Texas

Ann Richards became politically active while she was still a student at Baylor University in Austin, Texas. Early on, she joined the Young Democrats. She married David Richards, a lawyer, and spent several years raising their four children. Then, gradually, she moved into behind-the-scenes political work, supporting civil rights activists and the campaigns of women running for office, including Wilhemina Delco, the first African American woman elected to the Texas legislature.

In 1975 David was asked to run for Travis County commissioner, but he declined. Ann offered to stand in for him, and she was elected. She became the state treasurer of Texas in 1982, a move that gained her national attention. Throughout her career, Richards actively recruited women and minorities for important posts and continued her early focus on civil rights and social services.

In 1990 Richards entered the race for governor, one it seemed she couldn't win. Her Republican opponent, Clayton Williams, had power and money, but he also had an offensive manner. In the end, Richards's capable personality and her trademark sense of humor won the day. She lost her bid to retain her seat in 1994, a year when the Republicans swept the elections.

Mary Bourke Robinson (1944–)
President of Ireland

At the age of 25, Mary Robinson became the youngest person ever hired to teach law at Trinity College, Dublin, and in that same year won a seat in the *Seanad Éireann* (Irish Senate). She encouraged her fellow Irish to question many aspects of their traditional and conservative society. In Irish and European courts, she argued for women's legal rights on such issues as maternity benefits, day-care centers, birth control, and equal pay for equal work. Even though she was Roman Catholic, her criticism was frequently directed toward the church, especially concerning the issues of divorce and abortion.

A woman who spoke out on controversial issues in a male-dominated political arena, Robinson was triumphant when she was chosen the 1989 "Man of the Year" in her home county of Mayo. In 1990 she was nominated for president. Considered to have little chance of being elected, Robinson directed her campaign toward those who were usually not given much voice in Irish politics: women, the young, the poor, the unemployed, and the handicapped. She won by a narrow margin and claimed it as a victory for Irish women, "rocking the system instead of rocking the cradle."

From Irish Politics to Global Welfare

In July 1997, Mary Robinson entered the international political arena with her appointment as United Nations high commissioner for human rights. The United Nations was chartered in 1945 by the Allied powers—the United States, Soviet Union, Great Britain, and China—as a reaction to World War II. In addition to promoting peace, the UN is involved in areas such as environmental protection, economic and humanitarian aid to developing countries, and human rights. In her highly visible job as commissioner, Robinson coordinates the UN's human rights activities. She oversees investigations of violations worldwide and negotiates with the governments involved to resolve them.

Although in this mostly ceremonial role Robinson could no longer speak her mind as she had in the courtroom, she still served as a symbol for a changing Ireland, and, as she explained, "symbols can be extremely important." In 1997, in spite of her great popular support, she decided not to seek a second term as president. Instead, she moved on to work with the United Nations.

Eleanor Roosevelt (1884–1962)
First lady, social reformer

A REFORMER DEVOTED TO HUMAN RIGHTS, ELEANOR Roosevelt knew great sadness in her personal life. With gentle stubbornness she rose above private pain to achieve liberation, not only for herself, but for millions of others. She was the most active, influential, and admired first lady the United States has known.

An orphan by the time she was ten, Eleanor was raised by her grandmother, a cool and undemonstrative woman who soon sent the girl abroad for school. Eleanor entered society in her native New York City, as was expected of an upper-class young woman, but she found more satisfaction in social service work. In 1905 she married her distant cousin, Franklin Delano Roosevelt. At the ceremony, President Theodore Roosevelt—her uncle—gave her away. Eleanor found little happiness at home, which she had to share with her domineering mother-in-law, Sara. The Roosevelts became an effective political team, but their marriage was emotionally empty.

In 1910 Franklin ran successfully for the New York Senate, and Eleanor entered the political arena with him, battling her shyness to advance his candidacy. Throughout Franklin's long political career, Eleanor remained involved in causes such as women's rights, civil rights, health care, youth groups, housing, and employment. When he was paralyzed by polio in 1921, she became his legs and ears, traveling, speaking, and observing on his behalf.

Once Franklin was elected president in 1932, Eleanor began holding regular press conferences with women reporters, writing books and newspaper columns, and making radio broadcasts. Her responsibilities only increased after her husband's death in 1945. President Harry S. Truman named her as a delegate to the United Nations. In the last year of her life, she served as chairwoman of President John Kennedy's Commission on the Status of Women.

Nellie Tayloe Ross (1876–1977)
Governor of Wyoming

W HEN NELLIE TAYLOE ROSS'S HUSBAND, William, died in the middle of his term as governor of Wyoming, she was elected to serve the remaining two years, from 1925 to 1927. By a technicality, she can be said to be the first elected woman governor—Miriam "Ma" Ferguson won her gubernatorial election on the same day, but Ross was inaugurated two weeks earlier.

When Ross ran for reelection, she did not win, but she went on to pursue other political activities. She participated in presidential campaigns and served as vice-chairperson of the Democratic National Convention from 1928 to 1934. After she helped Franklin D. Roosevelt win the presidency, he appointed her director of the United States Mint in 1933. Again she was the first woman to hold that office.

At the time, the country was still in the grips of the Great Depression, so Ross had to contend with a heavy workload, made worse by a crippling lack of resources. Despite the obstacles, she supervised the mint with great skill for two decades, and was also appointed head of the Treasury Assay Committee, which tests the amount of metal in coins. The mint expanded considerably during Ross's time in office. She oversaw the construction of the United States gold depository at Fort Knox, the silver depository at West Point, and the new mint building in San Francisco.

Simone Rozès (1920–)
French Supreme Court justice,
international law expert

As a student at the University of Paris, Simone Rozès studied law with enthusiasm, although the idea of being a practicing lawyer did not appeal to her. Then in 1946, four years after her graduation, France passed a law allowing women to become judges. Rozès promptly took advantage of this newly opened door and embarked on her distinguished career.

Rozès began working for the Ministry of Justice in 1953. She went on to serve as a judge, vice president, and then president of the *Tribunal de grande instance* (Higher civil court). She had a long-standing interest in the legal systems of other countries and, for many years, was a member of the United Nations committee, which addressed crime prevention. In 1981 this focus led her to an appointment as a public prosecutor at the European Court of Justice, based in Luxembourg.

Rozès returned home in 1984 to serve on the *Court de cassation* (Supreme Court), where, as president, she was France's highest-ranking judge. Since her retirement in 1988, she remains as active as ever. She led a commission to explore solutions to corruption and how best to handle secrecy in criminal investigations in 1994.

Jeanne Benoît Sauvé (1922–1993)
Speaker of the House of Commons,
governor-general of Canada

Jeanne Sauvé belonged to the French-speaking Canadian minority, but she grew up in primarily English-speaking Ottawa. While she was at university there, she became involved in politics as a member of Jeunesse Étudiante Catholique (Young Catholic Students), a group committed to language reforms. During the 1950s and 1960s, Sauvé was a respected journalist, whose work appeared in newspapers and on television. Meanwhile her husband, Maurice, became a politician and spent several years in Parliament.

Sauvé also decided to enter politics and easily won a seat in the House of Commons in 1972. While there she became, in succession, secretary of state for science and technology, minister of the environment, and minister of communications. Her views on the importance of bilingualism, women's rights, education, and other liberal causes were known, but she pursued them with tactful diplomacy.

In 1980 Sauvé became the first woman to be named speaker of the House of Commons. For this difficult job, she maintained order and kept business moving in a heated, often combative atmosphere. She was pleased to leave the wrangling politicians behind in 1983 when she accepted another "first" for women: the job of governor-general, the official representative in Canada of the English monarch. She held the post until 1990.

Patricia Scott Schroeder (1940–)
United States congresswoman

In 1972 Pat Schroeder's husband, James, decided to become a campaign manager, but he needed a candidate to manage. As Schroeder later described it, she was the only person he could talk

Pat Schroeder often impressed supporters with her verbal wit. The inspiration for one of her most appreciated phrases struck while she was scrambling eggs one morning:

". . . when I looked down at the Teflon frying pan I was wiping clean, my face broke into a grin. That's what the Reagan presidency was like! Nothing stuck to it—not mounting deficits, trade imbalances, huge cuts in domestic programs, or even the scandals among the staff. Ronald Reagan was a Teflon-coated president. . . . later that day I trotted it out in a speech on the House floor. At least the term stuck—so to speak."

—PAT SCHROEDER
Champion of the Great American Family, 1989

into doing it. The odds were against her. She was a lawyer, not a politician, she had two small children, and she was running against a popular incumbent in Colorado, a state that had never sent a woman to the House of Representatives. Nevertheless, Schroeder, a Democrat, won the election, speaking out on such controversial issues as the need for stronger environmental protection, higher educational standards, and health-care reform, as well as her opposition to the Vietnam War.

Once in Congress, Schroeder made a point of joining the influential Armed Services Committee in order to challenge their habit of spending money on expensive technology and their resistance to opposing viewpoints. Hiring her own experts on budgets and weapons, she proposed sound alternatives. Although she lost her battles more often than not, she changed the attitude that the Pentagon could have whatever it wanted.

Known for her strong support of family issues, Schroeder was a major influence in the passage of the Family and Medical Leave Act of 1990. The law established situations—among them the illness of family members and the birth or adoption of children—in which employees must be allowed paid leave from their jobs. Schroeder retired from Congress in 1996, having been reelected 11 times.

Semiramis (9th century B.C.E.)
Queen of Assyria

DETAILS ABOUT THE LIFE OF SEMIRAMIS, OR Sammu-ramat, have been lost in the passage of time and distorted by the legends she inspired, but she is known to have existed. She was the wife of King Shamshi-Adad V of Assyria and ruled in her own right for three years after he died in 811 B.C.E. She became a heroine, known for her beauty and courage, who led her armies to conquer neighboring and distant countries and extended the boundaries of her landlocked country. A speech carved on a stone pillar that has been attributed to Semiramis declares, "No Assyrian before me had seen an ocean, but I have seen four."

Some sources credit Semiramis with building the city of Babylon and creating one of the Seven Wonders of the World there—the famous Hanging Gardens. Respected and feared during her life, she was worshiped after her death.

Donna Edna Shalala (1941–)
Government official, educator

DONNA SHALALA SHOWED TALENT FOR TAKING charge in a crisis quite early in life: When she was nine years old, a tornado touched down near her home in Cleveland, Ohio. Instead of running to take cover, though, Shalala marched to the street corner to direct traffic. As an adult she has continued to use these skills, first as a teacher, then in politics and academic administration.

In 1975 Shalala left her job as a political science professor at Columbia University to become director of the Municipal Assistance Corporation, established to save the nearly bankrupt New York City from financial ruin. Her success prompted President Jimmy Carter to make her assistant secretary of the Department of Housing and Urban Development in 1977. While there she made a point of promoting women's issues in housing.

Shalala returned to the academic world, becoming president of Hunter College in New York City in 1980 and chancellor of the University of Wisconsin at Madison in 1987. But President Bill Clinton convinced her to return to politics when he appointed her head of the Department of Health and Human Services in 1993.

Ruth Hanna McCormick Simms (1880–1944)
Illinois state congresswoman

MARK HANNA often took his daughter Ruth with him as he traveled to investigate labor disputes, masterminded political campaigns, and participated in Republican party meetings. He even made her his personal secretary when he was elected a United States senator and moved from Ohio to Washington, D.C. With this kind of apprenticeship, it is not surprising that Ruth became a notable politician herself.

A social progressive, Ruth became active in such organizations as the Women's Trade Union League and the National Child Welfare Association. Supporting her first husband, Joseph Medill McCormick, in his political career, she gained prominence in her own right. In 1919 she led the new women's executive committee of the Republican National Committee.

Ruth won a seat of her own, as Congressman-at-large for Illinois, in 1928. In this role, she gained respect as the most capable woman politician in the country: well-informed, eloquent, and witty. In 1930 she won the primary elections for the Senate, an achievement in itself, but ultimately lost to J. Hamilton Lewis, her Democratic opponent. Later, after marrying the New Mexico politician Albert Simms, Ruth participated in Thomas E. Dewey's unsuccessful campaigns for the presidency in 1944 and 1948.

Margaret Chase Smith (1897–1995)
United States congresswoman

MARGARET SMITH MOVED FROM MAINE TO Washington, D.C., when her husband, Clyde Smith, was elected to the United States House of Representatives in 1936. Having long served as his secretary, she was elected to take his place after he died four years later, and only age and ill health forced her to retire in 1972. During her multiple terms as representative and, after 1948, as senator, she was never swayed by anything but her own conscience, even when that meant voting against her fellow Republicans.

> "My creed is that public service must be more than doing a job efficiently and honestly. It must be a complete dedication to the people and to the nation with full recognition that every human being is entitled to courtesy and consideration, that constructive criticism is not only to be expected but sought, that smears are not only to be expected but fought, that honor is to be earned but not bought."
>
> —MARGARET CHASE SMITH
> "My Creed," 1953

In general, Smith was a liberal on domestic issues. She voted, along with the Democrats, in favor of most of Franklin Roosevelt's New Deal legislation. As Republican Senator Joseph McCarthy began his hunt for communist sympathizers in the late 1940s, Smith was the first member of the Republican party to speak out against his methods, both in the Senate and in her syndicated newspaper column. However, she was no supporter of communism if she felt that it threatened the country. Smith was a staunch believer in national security, and she advocated using nuclear weapons against the Soviet Union, if necessary. That stance won her the enmity of Soviet Premier Nikita Krushchev.

Smith was the daughter of a Maine barber who had not had the money to send her to college, but she gave herself an impressively effective education. She received dozens of honorary degrees and awards during her lifetime.

Soong Ch'ing-ling (1893–1981)
Chinese Nationalist, Madame Sun Yat-sen

Soong Mei-ling (1897–)
Chinese Nationalist, Madame Chiang Kai-shek

THE SOONG SISTERS PLAYED IMPORTANT ROLES IN 20th-century China, both as activists and as the wives of two very different political leaders. Both husbands were members of the Nationalist party, which eventually split, leaving them on opposite ends of the political spectrum—and bitter enemies.

The sisters' father, Charlie Soong, made a fortune selling Bibles and sent all his children to be educated in America. He was active in politics, supporting the nationalist movement that led to the overthrow of P'u-i, the last Chinese emperor, in 1911. Dr. Sun Yat-sen, whose leftist ideals inspired the revolution, became provisional president of the Republic, but continuing violence sent him—and the Soong family—into exile in Japan. There, he married Ch'ing-ling, despite her parents' disapproval. When they returned to Shanghai, Ch'ing-ling accompanied her husband in public appearances and continued to promote his ideals after he died in 1925. But Chiang Kai-shek, an extreme right-wing military leader, came to power and persecuted leftists such as Dr. Sun's followers.

Soong Mei-ling, Madame Chiang Kai-shek

Eager to use the Soong family wealth and influence to increase his military strength, Chiang Kai-shek married Mei-ling in 1927. Like her sister, Mei-ling participated in her husband's political activities. When he was held hostage, she personally gained his release. When he interrupted the civil war to defend the country from invasion by Japan, she sought support from the United States, where she became very popular. For a while, the Soong sisters worked together, but after the Chinese defeated Japan, the civil war resumed. While Mei-ling's husband made war, Ch'ing-ling struggled to help the victims, establishing hospitals and famine relief programs.

In 1949 the Chinese Communists took over and drove out Chiang and Mei-ling. Though not a Communist, Ch'ing-ling became a minister in the new government and eventually an honorary president. She remained active in the international peace movement, state affairs, and the welfare of women and children. She died before Mei-ling, who is still in exile.

Juanita Kidd Stout (1919–1998)
Pennsylvania Supreme Court justice

AFTER TEACHING SCHOOL IN HER NATIVE Oklahoma, Juanita Kidd Stout worked as a lawyer's secretary in Washington, D.C., and Philadelphia, then decided to become a lawyer herself. In 1948 she received her degree from Indiana University in Bloomington, fulfilling a childhood

dream. She was appointed Philadelphia assistant district attorney in 1956 and, three years later, became a Philadelphia County Court judge and the first black woman to be elected, rather than appointed, to the judge's bench.

Even as a teacher, Stout had believed in the importance of discipline as a part of learning. As a judge, she made a point of hearing juvenile delinquency cases promptly and making her rulings swift, tough, and sure. Her decisions were rarely reversed.

In 1988 Stout was inducted into the Pennsylvania Supreme Court, becoming the first African American woman to reach that level in a state legislative system. She had to step down a year later at the mandatory retirement age of 70 but went on to serve as senior judge in Philadelphia's Court of Common Pleas.

Hanna Suchocka (1946–)
Prime minister of Poland

HANNA SUCHOCKA FACED THE DIFFICULT TASK OF steering Poland toward capitalism as prime minister from July 1992 to October 1993. A lawyer who graduated from Poznan University in 1968, Suchocka was an expert on constitutional and human rights law. During the Communist era, she was active in the government, but she began to vote against the Communist party after martial law was declared in 1981. Three years later she was forced to resign because she refused to condemn Solidarity, a national workers' movement that demanded democratic reforms. The Communist government collapsed in 1989, and Suchocka was reelected with Solidarity's support.

The new parliamentary government, with its 29 different parties, was unstable. Suchocka was seen as a prime minister who could get things moving with a policy of compromise. At first she succeeded in improving the economy and instituting reforms, but the transition to a new economic system was painful. The Polish people were used to job security, if not freedom, and were unwilling to make sacrifices for promised future benefits. When Solidarity called for a vote of no-confidence, enough members of Parliament declared their lack of support for Suchocka that she was dismissed as prime minister. In the next elections she kept her seat, but her party, the Democratic Union, did not win the necessary majority for her to reclaim the office.

Helen Gavronsky Suzman (1917–)
Member of the South African Parliament

HELEN SUZMAN, THE DAUGHTER OF JEWISH Lithuanian immigrants, grew up near Johannesburg, South Africa. She attended the University of Witwatersrand and, during World War II, served as a statistician for the government. Her work brought to her attention the plight of nonwhites under apartheid, South Africa's official policy of discrimination against black, mixed-race, and Asian citizens. She became an economics professor and often expressed her concerns to her students.

In 1953 she entered politics, winning a seat in Parliament as a member of the moderate United party. Six years later she and 11 other politicians decided to make a stronger stand and formed the Progressive party to oppose racial segregation and repression. However, Suzman's colleagues were all defeated in the next elections.

Despite hostility from the white community, Suzman spoke out as a "minority of one." She condemned the lack of educational and economic opportunities for nonwhites and opposed the restrictions placed on them. During the 1970s the tide at last began to turn. Suzman retired from Parliament in

1989, the year before President F. W. de Klerk repealed most of the laws that had upheld apartheid. Within four years the government had been officially integrated, and the black activist Nelson Mandela had won the presidential elections.

Margaret Roberts Thatcher (1925–)
Prime minister of Great Britain

MARGARET ROBERTS, THE DAUGHTER OF A GROCER, grew up in the town of Grantham in Lincolnshire, England. She studied chemistry while in college at Oxford but became increasingly interested in politics. After her marriage to the businessman Denis Thatcher in 1951, she went on to get a law degree.

In 1959 Thatcher was elected to Parliament, and she rose steadily through the ranks of the Conservative party, becoming its leader in 1975. In the general election of 1979, she orchestrated her party's victory and became England's first female prime minister. She immediately enacted her program of Popular Capitalism, which involved dismantling the welfare state by reducing government spending and control, promoting a free economy, and cutting taxes. She placed a high value on hard work, strong defense, and breaking the powerful labor unions.

Although Thatcher succeeded in decreasing the national deficit and inflation, unemployment doubled, and riots broke out protesting the unfair burdens placed on the poor. However, she won praise from conservative voters, especially after she held out against Argentina in the struggle for control of the Falkland Islands. In the wake of this success, she called for an early election in 1983, winning a second term, then a third in 1987.

Parliament

England is governed by the parliamentary system, which consists of a monarch, the House of Lords, and the House of Commons. Originally the monarch was all-powerful. The House of Lords, which included church officials and people with titles, served as advisers. Property owners sent representatives to present their grievances to the monarch. Over time, that group of "commoners" took over England's government. The monarch is now a symbolic figure, and the Lords can refine laws but cannot prevent their passage. Members of the House of Commons are democratically elected. The leader of the political party that wins the most seats becomes the prime minister.

Dubbed the "Iron Lady," for her handling of foreign affairs during the Cold War, Thatcher also kept an iron grip on domestic affairs, until controversy within the Conservative party forced her resignation as prime minister in 1990. Two years later, she was made a baroness and took a seat in Parliament's House of Lords.

Theodora (497?–548)
Byzantine empress

THEODORA STARTED LIFE AS A PEASANT. ONE REPORT says that her father was a bear keeper at the circus in Constantinople, and she is known to have been an actress for a time. Her beauty won the heart of Justinian, the heir to the Byzantine throne; he

Economics, she studied high-tech industries and the global marketplace. That work and her book, *Who's Bashing Whom? Trade Conflict in High Technology Industries* (1992), attracted the attention of the newly elected president, Bill Clinton.

In 1993 Clinton named Tyson the head of his three-person Council of Economic Advisers. In this role, she explained and interpreted economic issues for the President, made forecasts, and helped plan policies. Two years later, Clinton promoted her to an even more important position, chair of the National Economic Council. Tyson remained in the post through 1996, then returned to Berkeley to resume her teaching career. During her time in Washington, she was praised for her expertise and down-to-earth avoidance of technical jargon. Some give her credit for the steady growth of the American economy.

changed a law forbidding marriage across class boundaries so they could wed in 525. They were crowned emperor and empress two years later and began a reign that was troubled by wars and invasions. During one revolt, in 532, Theodora prevented Justinian from fleeing and, by standing their ground, they defeated the rebels.

Brilliant and strong-willed, Theodora influenced every aspect of Byzantine government. She negotiated with diplomats, gave advice to foreign rulers, and drafted legislation. Her support for women was unprecedented. She passed laws protecting divorced women's property rights, forbidding the sale of children as slaves, and establishing harsh punishment for rape. After her death from cancer, Justinian was devastated. The remainder of his reign was undistinguished.

Tz'u-hsi (1835–1908)
Empress of China

Tz'U-HSI CONTROLLED CHINA FOR 50 YEARS, governing ably during the country's difficult transition from ancient traditions and isolation to modern ideas and trade with the West. Rumors of treachery and murder plagued her career, no doubt interlaced with truth.

Laura D'Andrea Tyson (1947–)
Presidential economic adviser

LAURA D'ANDREA TYSON, LOOKING TO COMBINE her talent at math with her interest in public policy, discovered economics when she was a student at Smith College. She earned her Ph.D. from the prestigious economics program at the Massachusetts Institute of Technology in 1974. Then she taught at Princeton and the University of California at Berkeley. As a member of the Berkeley Roundtable on International

Clever, ambitious Tz'u-hsi entered the court of Emperor Hsien-feng as a concubine. In 1856 she gave birth to the emperor's only son, T'ung-chih, and was elevated to empress. She joined forces with the emperor's mother and, when Hsien-feng died, they became coregents, roles typically played by men. Even after T'ung-chih came of age, his mother continued to rule through him—but he lived wildly and died at age 19. She then placed her sister's four-year-old son, Kuang-hsü, on the throne, breaking several rules of succession and maintaining her control.

In 1889 Tz'u-hsi retired amidst demands for an end to dynastic rule and the establishment of democracy. But when young Kuang-hsü attempted to institute reforms abruptly in 1898, his aunt returned and used military power to take over again. Tz'u-hsi was not opposed to reforms but believed they should happen gradually. The invasions and rebellions that ensued spelled the end of the monarchy. Although she attempted to direct China's destiny by naming the new emperor from her deathbed, P'u-i, her chosen successor, would be the last emperor.

Harriet Taylor Upton (1853–1945)
Republican party leader, women's rights activist, writer

HARRIET UPTON BEGAN LEARNING ABOUT POLITICS at an early age, accompanying her father, a Circuit Court judge in Ohio, as he traveled to hear cases and made speeches. He was elected to the House of Representatives in 1880, and she served as his official hostess. In this position, she met Republican party leaders and supporters of women's suffrage, a cause her father championed. Upton, however, held out against joining the suffragists because she felt men had always treated her as an equal. Then, in 1888, her preparatory research for an antisuffrage article inspired a change of heart. Upton became one of the country's most effective advocates of women's rights. She was a successful fund-raiser, a skilled debater, and a popular spokesperson.

In 1920 Upton was appointed vice-chair of the Republican National Executive Committee, a high-ranking political position. She used her influence to lobby on behalf of women's and children's welfare, especially regarding health and labor. In addition, Upton wrote novels, children's stories, historical accounts, and articles, often emphasizing political issues and women's role in history. Although Upton lost her bid to serve in Congress when she was 70, she worked in the administration of Governor Myers Cooper until she retired in 1931.

Agathe Uwilingiyimana (1953–1994)
Prime minister of Rwanda

THE SMALL AFRICAN NATION OF RWANDA HAS been devastated by violence between the minority Tutsis, who ruled as monarchs before Belgian colonization, and the majority Hutus, who seized power after independence was granted in 1962. Millions of Rwandans have died or fled the country. In 1992 an attempt was made to share control of the government. A former schoolteacher named Agathe Uwilingiyimana, a Tutsi, became minister of education and, the next year, prime minister, setting a precedent for Rwandan women to hold high government office.

In August 1993 Uwilingiyimana presided over negotiations for a coalition government with the Hutu-dominated party, the opposition parties, and the Tutsi rebels. The agreement meant Uwilingiyimana would lose her job when the government was restructured. Until the transition took place, she stayed on as caretaker. None of the plans were enacted. On April 6, 1994, panic broke out as the president and other top officials were assassinated, apparently by radical Hutus. The next day Uwilingiyimana's Rwandan guards murdered her, too, making her a victim of the ethnic hatred she had attempted to transcend and prolonging the violence still further.

Simone Jacob Veil (1927–)
President of the European Parliament

SIMONE VEIL'S ELECTION AS PRESIDENT OF THE European Parliament represents a great triumph for women and for Jews. During World War II, Veil and her family were deported to the Nazi concentration camp Auschwitz, along with thousands of other French Jews. With the same quiet determination that helped her survive the horrors of internment and losing her father, mother, and brother, Veil would later serve the people of Europe.

After the war Veil became a trial lawyer and then entered the Ministry of Justice. She rose through the ranks, helping draft liberal reforms, until President Valéry Giscard d'Estaing appointed her minister of health in 1974. Her calm, skillful arguments led to the passage of such controversial measures as an increase in social security taxes and the legalization of abortion and birth control. Opinion polls consistently named her the most popular political figure in France because of her competence and sincerity.

In 1979 Veil was elected to the European Parliament, defeating the energetic Jacques Chirac with her understated approach. The Parliament then elected her president, and she resigned from the French Cabinet to dedicate herself to her new responsibilities. She later returned to French government, serving as Minister of Health, Social Affairs, and Urban Affairs from 1993 to 1995. She remains active in politics and has played an influential role in the establishment of the European Union.

Victoria (1819–1901)
Queen of England

Q UEEN VICTORIA GAVE HER NAME TO AN ERA: The Victorian Age represents the values of stability and duty, but also prudery and extreme morality. At the beginning of her 64-year reign, the longest in the country's history, England was an island of farmers. By the time she died—just as the 20th century began—she ruled an industrial nation and an empire.

Victoria the woman was complex, both queenly and ordinary at the same time. She was stubborn, temperamental, and imperious, but also kind and generous. When told at age 11 that she would be queen, she promised to be good. After she was crowned at age 18, she devoted herself to her new role and its responsibilities, despite her youth. She had to learn to navigate the intricacies of English politics, but once she rose above the bickering of the opposing parties, she gained the respect and love of her people.

In 1839 Victoria met her cousin Albert and fell deeply in love. Their marriage was a successful one, both at home, where they produced nine children, and at court, where they shared royal duties. Victoria was so devastated by Albert's death in 1861 that she retreated from public life for three years and mourned him until the end of her life. But England was her second love, and she continued to exert her influence at home and in the ever-increasing colonies. She hated change, but the Industrial Revolution and its accompanying social reforms transformed England and the rest of the world.

Maxine Carr Waters (1938–)

United States congresswoman

MAXINE WATERS HAS FIRSTHAND EXPERIENCE OF the difficulties faced by the inner-city population. Growing up in St. Louis, Missouri, she was one of 13 children her mother raised alone, going on and off welfare. Waters married right after high school and had two children. By 1966 she was living in Los Angeles, California, barely getting by on low-paying jobs.

That year Waters was hired by Head Start, a federally sponsored educational program for underserved youth. Through teaching and supervising there, she became interested in politics and activism. In 1976 she was elected to the California State Assembly. For 14 years she vigilantly protected the interests of women and minorities. Her aggressive style offended some people, but she got things done. Among other issues, she supported legislation preventing policemen from strip-searching people arrested for minor offenses and persuaded the state government to withdraw its investments in South African businesses to protest apartheid.

Waters's success at passing important legislation made her a nationally recognized personality. She was elected to the House of Representatives by a large majority in 1990. Eight years later, during her third term in Washington, D.C., she was elected to chair the Congressional Black Caucus, an influential public policy group that is made up of African American representatives.

The L.A. Riots of '92

Maxine Waters played a key role when riots broke out in Los Angeles in 1992. An African American man named Rodney King had been beaten by white police officers, an incident that was captured on videotape and shown on televisions across the country. When the matter came to trial, though, an all-white jury acquitted the accused officers. That decision was met with outrage. Riots paralyzed the city for five days. While never justifying the violence, Waters spoke out on behalf of the rioters, pointing out that hopeless social and economic conditions drove them to use such terrible methods of protest.

Alice Stebbins Wells (1873–1957)

Policewoman

ALICE WELLS, WHO WAS BORN IN MANHATTAN, Kansas, began as a theologian and Congregational preacher. After moving to Los Angeles, California, where she engaged in prison reform, she became convinced the world needed women police officers because they "could help in many ways where men would be powerless." Wells was not trying to achieve equality with men; she shared the common belief of her day that women were more capable than men of exerting a beneficial moral influence on society.

In 1910 she convinced the city of Los Angeles to create the country's first department for policewomen and became the first recruit. But she didn't stop there: she lectured on the importance of policewomen to international audiences, started departments in other cities, formed organizations such as the International Association of Policewomen, and taught the first university training class for policewomen. She was a petite woman with a "sweet smile and low voice." At first people who encountered her on duty thought she had borrowed her husband's badge. But then she was given a new one with "Police Woman's Badge #1" printed on it in big letters.

Christine Todd Whitman (1946–)

Governor of New Jersey

GOVERNOR CHRISTINE TODD WHITMAN'S SUCCESS in handling New Jersey's $2 billion deficit has made her one of the country's most admired Republican politicians, but many people were surprised that she was elected at all. Her critics felt she lacked experience. Her family wealth made her seem removed from the ordinary voter. And she made several public relations blunders during her campaign, among them announcing plans to hire Larry McCarthy, a consultant who created an ad for George Bush's presidential campaign that many black voters considered racist. But Whitman promised to cut taxes. The incumbent governor, Jim Florio, had recently raised them drastically.

Whitman was not completely inexperienced about politics. Her parents, Webster and Eleanor Todd, were active Republicans; and her husband, John, is the grandson of former New York governor Charles Whitman. She herself served on the Somerset County Board of Chosen Freeholders, a local governing body, for five years. In 1990 she lost a bid for a seat in the Senate to Democrat Bill Bradley, but only by a small margin. The race for governor in 1994 was characterized by accusations on both sides, but Whitman beat Florio, cut taxes as promised, and won reelection in 1997. Many people predict that she will run for president one day.

Wilhelmina I (1880–1962)
Queen of the Netherlands

UNTIL THE NETHERLANDS WAS INVADED BY Germany in 1940, Queen Wilhelmina had succeeded in keeping her country at peace for 42 years. Even during World War I, with the disruption of trade, food shortages, and refugees flooding into the country, she had preserved her country's neutrality and prevented revolution.

Wilhelmina, who ruled jointly with the Dutch Parliament, had a gift for diplomacy and administration. She helped to improve the nation's economy and to establish the capital city of The Hague as a meeting place for international decision-makers. In person she was somewhat restrained—she had had a very strict, genteel upbringing—but she was adored by her people. She was often seen bicycling around the city in comfortable, old clothes.

After surrendering under protest to the Germans and fleeing to London, Queen Wilhelmina became a symbol of resistance, encouraging her people through radio broadcasts. She returned home after the war and helped arrange for the Netherlands to become a charter member of the United Nations, even though this meant giving up the country's neutral status. In 1948 she passed the crown to her daughter, Juliana.

Ivy Williams (1877–1966)
Barrister

IVY WILLIAMS, THE DAUGHTER OF A SOLICITOR IN Oxford, England, knew that she wanted to follow in her father's footsteps, but her chosen career in law required her to be patient. At the time, women were allowed to attend classes and take examinations at Oxford University, but they were not awarded degrees. When Williams took the exams in 1902, she passed them with flying colors.

Nearly two decades later, in 1920, women were given full membership to Oxford University and admitted to the Inns of Court. At last in possession of her degree, Wells joined the Inner Temple, one of the four English legal societies. Two years later she became the first woman to be called to the English bar. Rather than setting up a law practice, Williams chose to inspire young women law students. She worked as a tutor and lecturer at Oxford until 1945.

In later years, Williams's eyesight began to fail. Then, she devoted herself to the study and teaching of Braille, a special alphabet that is read by running the tips of the fingers over small, raised dots embossed onto paper.

Bertha Wilson (1923–)
Canadian Supreme Court justice

BERTHA WILSON WAS BORN IN SCOTLAND AND moved to Canada with her husband, Reverend John Wilson, when she was in her mid-20s. By 1954 they had settled in Halifax, Nova Scotia, where she sought admission to law school. But the dean at Dalhousie University was skeptical. "Why don't you just go home and take up crocheting?" he asked.

Wilson eventually convinced the dean that she was a serious student, and she embarked on a career that would lead to her recognition as one of the best legal scholars of her day. From 1959 to 1975, Wilson practiced at a large Toronto law firm, becoming both partner and queen's counsel. She left there when she was appointed to the Ontario Court of Appeal. In 1982 she was the first woman called to the Canadian Supreme Court. It was a time when the court was expanding in influence and power, because England had only recently granted the colony full self-governing status.

Respected for her rigorous legal analysis and her belief that the law must be humane, Wilson has received many honors. Wilson retired in 1991 but continues to influence changes within the legal profession as a member of the Canadian Bar Association's Task Force on Gender Equality in the Legal Profession and of the Royal Commission on Aboriginal Peoples.

handwriting on official documents—although she was intelligent, Edith had had little formal schooling. Wilson's term ended in 1921 and, following his death a few years later, Edith devoted herself to keeping his memory alive.

Edith Bolling Galt Wilson (1872–1961)
First lady of the United States

President Woodrow Wilson was a sad and lonely widower when he met Edith Galt in 1915. He fell in love immediately with this attractive widow, who came from an old Virginia family that claimed Pocahontas as an ancestor. They were married nine months later. Edith made the White House a lively place with her warmth and charm. She also became a trusted adviser to her husband, accompanying him on his successful reelection campaign, sharing his work, and letting him know her opinions. Rarely apart, the couple traveled to Paris in 1919—just after World War I—to support the establishment of an international peace-keeping force known as the League of Nations, a precursor to the United Nations.

When Woodrow Wilson suffered a serious stroke later that year, the government almost ground to a halt. Convinced that resignation would deprive her husband of his will to go on living, Edith took on an unprecedented number of his tasks, refusing all outside help. She could not prevent the public from becoming suspicious, though. One of the things that made people uneasy was the appearance of her poor

Wu Chao (625–705)
Empress of China

It's hard to say which quality makes Wu Chao most notable: her success in attaining the highest position in a land where women's status was low, her success at governing, or her successful destruction of anyone who got in her way. Wu Chao, also known as Wu Tse-T'ien, became the only woman to rule China in her own right. She worked her way up from concubine to Emperor Kao Tsung, to his favorite wife, to empress. The elderly emperor became progressively sicker and weaker, leaving his responsibilities to her. After he died, she kept control of the country by deporting one of her sons, Chung, and ruling through his less competent brother, Jui. During her reign, she achieved peace and prosperity through diplomacy and popular reforms. Culture and the arts thrived.

However, Wu Chao was also thoroughly unscrupulous. She eliminated anyone—even her own family

The T'ang Dynasty

Wu Chao came to power during one of the most remarkable periods in Chinese history, the T'ang dynasty, which began in 618 and faded from power around 907. The T'ang dynasty is especially known as a time when the arts flowered. New poetic verse forms were introduced; painters became celebrities, their work patronized by the royal court; and new pottery finishes were invented. In keeping with her lust for power, the Empress Wu tried to proclaim a new dynasty of her own—the Chou dynasty— but the designation did not stick. The T'ang resumed after her death and reached its golden age not long afterward.

members—who might possibly pose a threat to her power. She ruled until she was nearly 75 years old, then brought Chung back from exile and made him emperor.

Zenobia (3rd century)
Queen of Palmyra

THE EMPIRE THAT ZENOBIA ASSEMBLED IN THE eastern Mediterranean challenged the Roman Empire, the greatest power on Earth at the time. At first she ruled by the side of her husband, King Odaenathus of Palmyra. She was never satisfied with playing second fiddle, though. Allegedly she had her husband and his heir by a first wife killed, then ruled through her own son, Wahballat. An effective and dramatic queen, she wrote histories, hunted panthers, and rode on a warhorse into battle.

However, Palmyra (in present-day Syria) was a Roman colony, and Zenobia held power only by permission of the Roman authorities. Determined to change that, she made excursions into Egypt and Asia Minor in 269, conquering nations or making them her allies. This soon got the attention of the Roman emperor, Aurelian, who used his mightiest forces against her. Zenobia was captured and taken back to Rome for exhibition in the triumphal procession. But her fate was not a tragic one—she was granted a villa, along with a pension, and eventually became a Roman senator's wife.

Khaleda Zia (1945–)
Prime minister of Bangladesh

FORMER HOMEMAKER KHALEDA ZIA BECAME prime minister of Bangladesh in 1991. Her task was a difficult one: the country is plagued by poverty, disease, devastating tropical storms, and continuing civil disturbance. During the 14th century, the area was a part of an independent nation called Bengal, and under British rule it became the eastern region of Pakistan. After Bangladesh became an independent nation in 1971, one military leader after another had attempted to rule as dictator, bringing about corruption and assassinations.

Khaleda's husband, Zia ur-Rahman, had been at the forefront of the fight for liberation. He became president in 1977, and although he established order and won public support, he was still a military dictator. He was assassinated in 1981 and succeeded by Hossain Mohammad Ershad.

Zia, as chair of the Bangladesh Nationalist party, fought a determined campaign against Ershad for years, leading public demonstrations to demand the restoration of democracy and civil rights. Her goal was achieved when Ershad resigned in 1990. The BNP won the majority in the ensuing election, making Zia prime minister. She did much to modernize her country, promoting economic growth, environmental policies, women's rights, and universal literacy. But the civil unrest continued. She was defeated in the 1996 elections by another woman leader and her longtime rival, Sheik Hajina Wased.

T I M E   L I N E

1500 B.C.E.	Hatshepsut, Egypt's first female pharaoh, rules peacefully for 20 years.
9th century B.C.E.	Queen Semiramis reigns in Assyria.
6th century B.C.E.	The first books of the Old Testament of the Bible are recorded.
500 B.C.E.	Queen Artemisia helps Xerxes, ruler of the Persian Empire, in his attack on the Greeks.

Queen Artemisia I of Halicarnassus

51 B.C.E.	Cleopatra and her brother Ptolemy XIII become corulers of Egypt.
1st century	The books of the New Testament of the Bible are recorded.
49	Agrippina II, the younger, marries the Emperor Claudius, at last achieving the power for which she has long been scheming.
61	The warrior queen Boudicca leads her army of Britons in rebellion against the Romans.

260	Upon the death of her husband, Zenobia becomes the sole ruler of Palmyra in Syria.
470	Fall of the Roman Empire
548	The brilliant, progressive Empress Theodora dies in Constantinople, and her grief-stricken husband, Justinian, accomplishes little of note in what remains of his reign.
550	Brunhilde rules the Frankish Kingdom in Austrasia for 40 years.
650	Empress Wu Chao assumes control of China. She rules for half a century.
680	Empress Jito becomes ruler of Japan after her husband's death.
1130	Eleanor of Aquitaine becomes the queen of France when she marries King Louis VII.
1150	Having ended her marriage to Louis, Eleanor of Aquitaine marries King Henry VI and becomes the queen of England.
1226	Blanche of Castile becomes regent for her son, Louis IX, after her husband's death.
1337–1453	The Hundred Years' War between England and France
1388	Margaret, already queen of Denmark and Norway, is crowned queen of Sweden as well, bringing the three countries together in what is called the Kalmar Union.

1469	Queen Isabella of Castile marries King Ferdinand II of Aragon, uniting their two Spanish kingdoms.
1492	Explorer Christopher Columbus lands on San Salvador, an island in the Bahamas, and claims this New World in the name of the Spanish King Ferdinand.
1533	Catherine de Médicis marries Henri de Valois, later to be King Henri II of France.
1534	King Henry VIII founds the Church of England and separates from the Roman Catholic Church.
1551	Mary I becomes queen of England.
1558–1603	Elizabeth I rules England.
1587	In England Mary Queen of Scots is tried for conspiring to kill Queen Elizabeth, found guilty, and executed.
1645	The intellectual Queen Christina of Sweden establishes the first Swedish newspaper.

Queen Christina of Sweden

1663	Queen Nzinga of Ndongo rules in Angola after the death of her brother.
1740	The mother of Marie Antoinette, Maria Theresa, becomes queen of Hungary and Bohemia.
1762	Catherine the Great, the empress of Russia, begins her reign. She will rule for 34 years.
1775–1783	The American Revolution. The Declaration of Independence is signed in July 1776.
1789–1799	Revolution in France
1848	The first women's rights convention is held in Seneca Falls, New York.
1851	Prince Albert, husband of Queen Victoria of England, sponsors the Crystal Palace Exhibition to display the technological wonders of the Industrial Revolution. The grand showcase is often considered to encapsulize the greatness of the Victorian Age.
1857	Indian hero Lakshmi Bai, the Rani of Jhansi, leads a revolt against the British.
1862	Ruling through the weaker men who rightfully inherit the throne, Empress Tz'u-hsi begins her sporadic and lengthy control of China.
1865	The 13th Amendment to the United States Constitution is ratified by Congress. It prohibits slavery or any other denial of freedom without due process of law.
1869	At the encouragement of future Justice of the Peace Esther Morris, the politicians of Wyoming Territory pass a bill that gives women the right to vote. It is still a good half-century before the federal government follows suit.

1891   Queen Liliuokalani, the last monarch of Hawaii, begins her brief reign.

1914–1918   World War I. Dorothy Peto, an aspiring policewoman, promptly takes advantage of the men's absence and volunteers to serve on a British police force.

1919   Lady Nancy Astor becomes the first woman member of Great Britain's Parliament.

In Germany, partly as the result of the work of such activists as the country's first woman lawyer, Anita Augspurg, women are granted the right to vote.

1920   The 19th Amendment to the United States Constitution grants women the vote. It goes into effect August 26th.

1923   Katherine, dutchess of Atholl, becomes the first Scottish woman to serve in the British Parliament.

1924   Two women win state elections to share the honor of being America's first female governors: Nellie Tayloe Ross of Wyoming and Miriam Ferguson of Texas.

1932   Hattie Caraway of Arkansas takes the seat of her late husband in the United States Senate.

Eleanor Roosevelt becomes first lady after her husband wins the presidential race.

1939–1945   World War II. Katherine, the duchess of Atholl and a former member of the British Parliament, translates Adolf Hitler's autobiography, *Mein Kampf* (My Struggle), into English, hoping to warn people of the dangers of fascism.

1941   On December 8th, Congresswoman Jeannette Rankin casts a lone vote opposing the United States' declaration of entry in to World War II. She is the only member of Congress to have voted against both world wars.

Jeannette Rankin

1947   England withdraws from its Indian colonies. The area separates into two independent countries, predominantly Hindu India and Muslim Pakistan.

1948   In South Africa, the National Party comes to power. Within a year a new official policy of racial segregation called apartheid is announced.

Israel is declared an independent country, sparking conflict between the Jews, who have settled there, and the Palestinians, many of whom must be displaced.

1949   The Communist Revolution in China. Right-wing leader Chiang Kai-shek and his wife, Soong Mei-ling, are forced into exile.

1950–1953   The Korean War. In an effort to prevent the expansion of communism in the area, the United States and the United Nations join the fighting on the side of the South Koreans.

1951	Eva Perón declares her candidacy for vice president of Argentina despite objections from the military.
1952	Elizabeth II inherits the British throne after the death of her father.
1959	Indira Ghandi is elected president of the Indian Congress party.
	Clare Boothe Luce is appointed ambassador to Brazil but resigns after receiving criticism from Senator Wayne Morse of Oregon.
1960	Governor General Oliver Goonetilleke of Ceylon appoints Sirimavo Bandaranaike prime minister of the island country, even though she was not a candidate for a seat in the parliamentary elections. This procedure for filling the position is unprecedented.
1964–1975	War in Vietnam. The United States enters the conflict as an ally of South Vietnam, battling Communist forces in the North.
1965	Barbara Jordan is elected to the Texas Senate.
1968	Shirley Chisholm, the first black woman elected to Congress, begins the first of her seven terms in the House of Representatives.
1969	Golda Meir is sworn in as Israel's first female prime minister.
	Twenty-one-year-old Irish politician and activist, Bernadette Devlin, becomes the youngest woman elected to the British parliament.
1973	President Richard Nixon resigns in the wake of the Watergate scandal, and Gerald and Betty Ford move into the White House.

1974	After the death of her husband, Isabel Perón succeeds him as the president of Argentina.
	Elizabeth Domitien is appointed prime minister of the Central African Republic.
1975	Shirley Temple Black is appointed United States ambassador to Ghana.
1976	For the first time ever, female cadets are admitted to the United States Military Academy at West Point and to the United States Air Force Academy at Colorado Springs, Colorado.

Patricia Roberts Harris

1977	President Jimmy Carter appoints Illinois lawyer Patricia Roberts Harris Secretary of Housing and Urban Development. Two years later, Harris is named Secretary of Health, Education, and Welfare.
1979	The Islamic Revolution. Under the leadership of the Ayatollah Khomeini, Islamic fundamentalists seize control of the Iranian government. As a result, stateswoman Mahnaz Afkhami is forced to relinquish her posts.
	Margaret Thatcher becomes the first woman prime minister of Great Britain.

1980   Vigdis Finnbogadóttir of Iceland becomes the world's first woman to be made head of state by a democratic election.

1981   Sandra Day O'Connor is sworn in as the first female Supreme Court justice in the United States.

Gro Harlem Brundtland is elected the first woman prime minister of Norway.

1982   England grants its colony Canada self-governing status. It becomes a parliamentary democracy.

1984   Prime Minister Indira Gandhi of India is assassinated by her Sikh guards.

Democratic presidential hopeful Walter Mondale chooses Geraldine Ferraro as his running mate. Although they lose the election, Ferraro's strong stand as a vice-presidential candidate inspires many women.

1985   Native American Wilma Mankiller becomes chief of the Cherokee Nation of Oklahoma.

1986   Corazon Aquino is elected president of the Philippines amid accusations of ballot-tampering by Ferdinand Marcos.

1988   Ann Richards, future governor of Texas and keynote speaker at the Democratic National Convention, makes headlines by quipping that Republican presidential candidate, George Bush, was "born with a silver foot in his mouth."

Benazir Bhutto takes office as prime minister of Pakistan. She is the first woman to head a Muslim nation.

1989   The Cold War ends. In Germany, the Berlin Wall is torn down, and the country is reunited.

1990   Ertha Pascal-Trouillot becomes the first woman to sit on the Supreme Court of Haiti.

Violeta Barrios de Chamorro is elected president of Nicaragua.

1991   Burmese opposition leader Aung San Suu Kyi is awarded the Nobel Peace Prize but is unable to travel to Stockholm, Sweden, to accept it, because she is under house arrest.

1992   Riots erupt in Los Angeles after white police officers are acquitted for the beating of Rodney King, an African American. Congresswoman Maxine Waters speaks on behalf of the rioters.

1993   Kim Campbell becomes the first female prime minister of Canada.

Tansu Çiller becomes the first female prime minister of Turkey.

Lawyer and feminist Ruth Bader Ginsburg is appointed to the Supreme Court of the United States.

1994   Agathe Uwilingiyimana, interim prime minister of Rwanda, is assassinated when the ethnic violence that has long plagued the country breaks out once again.

1995   Women representatives from 185 countries gather in Beijing, China, for the Fourth World Conference on Women. Among them are Benazir Bhutto and Hillary Clinton.

1997   Former Irish president Mary Robinson accepts a post at the United Nations as High Commissioner of Human Rights.

1998   Former New York congresswoman and outspoken activist Bella Abzug dies.

G L O S S A R Y

AFL–CIO: the American Federation of Labor–Congress of Industrial Organizations; a merger of two labor organizations that was formed in 1955 to promote the interests of American workers in crafts and industrial unions.

Ambassador: a high-ranking official sent as a diplomat to represent his or her country's government in a foreign land.

Annex: to attach or claim a smaller territory as part of a larger one, often by force.

Assassinate: to kill someone, most often a public figure, and usually for political reasons.

Barrister: in England, a lawyer who is permitted to practice in the higher courts, those that deal with more serious cases.

Cabinet: a group of officially appointed advisers to a prominent leader, such as a president or governor.

Civil rights: rights and political freedoms granted to citizens. Designed to provide for equal legal, economic, and social treatment under the law.

Communism: a political theory of social organization in which all property, industrial concerns, and the means of production are owned collectively by the public.

Concubine: a mistress or, in polygamous societies where multiple wives are permitted, a wife who has inferior social status.

Congress: the national legislative body of the United States that includes the House of Representatives and the Senate.

Conservative: tending to favor established, traditional institutions and values.

Deficit: a lack or shortfall. The word is often used in connection with budgets to describe the amount by which the projected expenses of a government or institution exceed the amount of money available to pay for them.

Democracy: a form of government in which power is held either by the people themselves, or by their elected representatives.

Despot: a leader who possesses unlimited power over his or her subjects and who exercises that authority tyrannically.

Dictator: a leader who exercises absolute power with unrestricted authority; dictators are often—but not always—despotic.

Diplomacy: the conduct of negotiations between separate nations; the government officers engaged in diplomacy are known as diplomats.

Dynasty: a succession of rulers who descend from the same family and who reach the throne by inheriting it.

Empire: a territory that is controlled by a leader (called an emperor or empress) who holds absolute power.

Fascism: a political philosophy that holds national supremacy and racial unity to be more important than individual rights.

Genocide: the systematic slaughter of an ethnic, political, or religious group.

Gubernatorial: having to do with the office of governor.

Lobbying: the practice of actively promoting a cause or project to representatives of the government in hopes of influencing legislation that is beneficial to that cause.

Maharaja: a Hindu noble of high rank, usually translated as "prince." Before India was declared a democracy, the individual states that made up the country were ruled by maharajas.

Martial law: military rule imposed on an area when civil rule has broken down, as during a war.

Military coup: the sudden and forceful overthrow of a government, dictator, or other ruling body by the military.

Monarchy: a form of government by which a country is governed by a ruler (the monarch) who has achieved his or her position by inheriting it.

Nationalism: loyalty to one nation or cultural group above any other.

New Deal: a program enacted by President Franklin Roosevelt during the 1930s created to promote social reform and to speed economic recovery from the Depression.

Pharaoh: the title used by the rulers of ancient Egypt.

Plenipotentiary: having been vested with complete authority to represent a group or government. Used most often to describe an ambassador.

Political asylum: sanctuary or protection offered by one government to people persecuted by another government for political reasons.

President: literally, a leader who *presides* over a group of people or a business. In American politics, the president is the elected leader of the nation.

Prime minister: the elected head of a government under the parliamentary system.

Progressive: one who supports moderate political change that advances social reform.

Protocol: the code of ceremonial forms that are considered proper in official interactions, especially between diplomats or heads of state.

Purdah: the practice among Muslims and (less commonly) among Hindus, in which the women are required to stay out of public view, often in special women's quarters.

Reformatory: an institution where young people or women who are convicted of relatively minor crimes are sent, in hopes that they can be reformed and returned to society.

Regent: the person who is designated to rule a country or territory during the absence of a monarch, or until a child ruler is of age.

Republic: a state or nation governed by an elected leader (usually called a president), a group of elected officials, or both.

Socialism: a theory of social organization in which the means of production are owned and administered by the state, not by individual citizens.

Solicitor: in England, a lawyer who advises clients, prepares case materials for barristers, and pleads cases in the lower courts.

Tory: a term that has been applied to different groups in British history. Since the late 17th century, the Tories have been a major political party in England, and their opposition has been the Liberal, or Labor, party. In 1830 the Tories began calling themselves the Conservatives.

Tribute money: money paid regularly by a local ruler to a more powerful ruler. The tribute might be paid to prevent a smaller kingdom from being attacked by a larger one or to preserve a certain amount of local autonomy.

UNESCO: the United Nations Educational, Scientific, and Cultural Organization. A special agency of the United Nations that was established in 1946 and designed to promote peace through international cooperation in educational, scientific, and cultural projects.

INDEX

Numbers in boldface type indicate main entries.

CREDITS

Quotes

8 Adams, Abigail. *Letters of Mrs. Adams, the Wife of John Adams, with an Introductory Memoir by Her Grandson, Charles Francis Adams. Vol. I.* Boston: Charles C. Little and James Brown, 1811. 12 Astor, Nancy. *My Two Countries.* London: William Heinemann Ltd., 1923. 33 Harris, Mary B. *I Knew Them in Prison.* New York: The Viking Press, 1936. 34 Lichtheim, Miriam (editor). *Ancient Egyptian Literature, Volume II: The New Kingdom.* Berkeley, CA: University of California Press, 1976. Used by permission. 40 Lyons, Enid, Dame. *Among the Carrion Crows.* Adelaide: Rigby Limited, 1972. Used by permission. 54 Josephson, Hannah. *Jeannette Rankin: First Lady in Congress.* Indianapolis: Bobbs-Merrill, 1974. 59 Schroeder, Pat (with Andrea Camp and Robyn Lipner). *Champion of the Great American Family.* New York: Random House, 1989. Used by permission. 60 Smith, Margaret Chase. "My Creed," from *Quick* magazine, November 11, 1953 © Triangle Publications, 1953. Used by permission.

Photographs

Abbreviations

AP   AP Wide World Photos
COR   Corbis
HG   Hulton Getty
LOC   Library of Congress

8 Abzug, Bella, LOC. 9 Agrippina the Younger, LOC. 10 Allen, Florence Ellinwood, LOC. 11 Aquino, Corazon, AP. 12 Atholl, Katherine, Duchess, LOC. 13 Aung San Suu Kyi, AP. 15 Bhutto, Benazir, AP; Black, Shirley Temple HG. 16 (and 6) Bolin, Jane, LOC. 17 Boudicca, HG. 18 Byrne, Jane, AP. 19 Caraway, Hattie, LOC. 21 Chiang Ch'ing, HG. 22 Chisholm, Shirley, COR/Bettmann. 23 Cleopatra VII, HG. 24 (and 7) Clinton, Hillary, LOC. 25 Devlin, Bernadette, HG. 26 Elizabeth I, HG. 27 Elizabeth II, photography by Roger Cooper/National Archives of Canada/PA-141503. 28 (and title page) Fauset, Crystal Bird, LOC. 29 Felton, Rebecca, LOC. 30 Finnbogadóttir, Vigdis, Office of the President, Iceland; Ford, Elizabeth. LOC. 31 (and cover) Gandhi, Indira, HG. 32 Harriman, Pamela, COR/Bettmann. 33 Harvard, Beverly, courtesy of the Atlanta Police Department. 35 Hobby, Oveta Culp, LOC. 35 (and title page) Isabella I, HG. 36 (and 7) Jordan, Barbara, LOC. 38 Krupskaya, Nadezhda, HG. 39 (and 6) Liliuokalani, LOC. 40 Luce, Clare Boothe, LOC. 41 Mankiller, Wilma, Yale University Office of Public Information. 42 Maria Theresa, HG. 43 Mary, Queen of Scots, HG. 44 Meir, Golda, LOC; Mesta, Perle, LOC. 45 Mink, Patsy, LOC. 47 Myerson, Bess, LOC. 47 (and title page) Myrdal, Alva, LOC. 48 Nguyen Thi Binh, LOC. 49 O'Connor, Sandra Day, LOC. 50 (and title page) Perkins, Frances, LOC. 51 (and cover) Perón, Eva, HG. 52 Peterson, Esther, LOC. 54 Pompadour, Jeanne, Marquise de, HG. 55 Ray, Dixy Lee, LOC. 56 Richards, Ann, Texas Governor's Office. 57 (and cover) Roosevelt, Eleanor, LOC. 58 Ross, Nellie, LOC. 59 Semiramis, LOC. 60 Simms, Ruth, LOC. 61 Soong Mei-ling, LOC. 62 Stout, Juanita Kidd, LOC. 63 Suzman, Helen, HG. 64 (and cover) Theodora, Empress, HG. 64 Tz'u-hsi, LOC. 66 Veil, Simone, HG; Victoria, Queen, LOC. 68 Wilhelmina I, Queen, HG. 69 Wilson, Edith, LOC. 70 Zenobia, HG. 71 Artemisia, LOC. 72 Christina, Queen of Sweden, HG. 73 Rankin, Jeanette, LOC. 74 Harris, Patricia Roberts, LOC.